FINANCIAL PLANNING
AND DEBT MANAGEMENT

How To Plan A Successful Life

TONY GIGGS

Table of Contents

INTRODUCTION

I want to thank you and congratulate you for downloading the book, *"Financial Planning and Debt Management: How to plan a successful life"*.

This book carefully details on how you can use your finances to become happy and prosperous in what you do. We will look at what it entails to have financial prosperity and freedom.

What is financial prosperity? How do you know you are living in financial prosperity? What makes you successful in your finances? Are financial prosperity and financial freedom the same?

Many people wish they could:

1. Make a lot of money

2. Pay off my debts

3. Go on vacation

4. Buy some good staff

5. Own/rent a home

All these are very important questions you need to answer as an individual before you say you have financial prosperity. Truth be told, the standard definition of financial prosperity and financial freedom that cuts across the board has nothing to do with how much money you earn or how much is in your bank, or how much you spend. Now, let us define financial freedom then define financial prosperity.

Financial Freedom is the ability of an individual to take charge of his or her finances. If I ask you, is your money controlling you or are you the one controlling your money? If you are the one controlling your finances then you have financial freedom, if your finances are controlling you then you need to reconsider. This means an individual might be getting $100 but that person has financial freedom and one who earns $1000 has no financial freedom.

Financial Prosperity is the ability of an individual to live within their financial capability. This means you comfortably live within your financial capability. Do you tend to overspend and end up with frustrations? Then you don't have financial prosperity. As I said the standard definition has nothing to do with the income that one earns.

The best gift you can give yourself when it comes to finances is by you being able to control your own finance and living in accordance with your standards.

You can have all the wealth and financial prosperity in your life that you want by using the law of attraction. The basic concept for attracting wealth and prosperity is rather simple.

All thoughts create in some way, positive thoughts will create positive situations and negative thoughts will create negative situations. Most people have a combination of positive and negative thoughts mixed throughout the day.

Some simple steps in using the law of attraction to create financial prosperity in your life.

Give earnest heartfelt thanks for the things, people and situations that come into your life. If you find yourself in a seemingly negative situation, give thanks for the opportunity to learn from it. When you pull out a bill to buy anything give thanks for the financial prosperity you received in having that bill. You do not have to believe in God, you can give thanks to the universe or whatever suits your personality.

Put a $20.00 dollar bill (any denomination will do, your choice) in your pocket and play a game with it. Everywhere you go pretend you are spending that money on different things you want. You can spend that money a thousand times in a day. As you spend the money, give thanks for the wealth and prosperity that is yours and the ability to be able to spend the money.

Watch your thoughts closely for negative thoughts creeping in. If you want to use the law of attraction for attracting financial prosperity you must watch for those negative thoughts. One simple way to break the pattern of negative thoughts is to find things you like and can be thankful for. As an example, if you were walking down the street, find something you like about everyone you pass and give thanks for that item. You could say "thank you for that man who has the courage to wear a pink shirt". You can say "thank you for the beautiful shoes that lady is wearing".

Believe in yourself and the fact that this will work for you. Practice the above exercises every day and watch for signs of financial prosperity flowing into your life. At first, you may see a trickle of wealth and prosperity, as you start seeing results and your belief increases you will start seeing more and more. Have fun and keep practicing the exercises to achieve wealth and financial prosperity.

Thanks again for downloading this book, I hope you enjoy it!

CHAPTER 1

UNDERSTANDING FINANCIAL PROSPERITY AND FREEDOM

There are some basic needs we all have as individuals that need to be met. At the top of the list are the needs necessary for survival - food, clothing, and shelter. These basic needs can be met with ease when one has financial prosperity to meet those needs.

The focus is to be able to meet our daily needs. Jesus never went around with a lot of money (although he did have a treasurer. Broke people don't need treasurers). He also knew that he would be able to meet every need that arose because he walked in financial prosperity. He knew how to meet needs once they arose.

Here are some ideas on what it means to walk in financial prosperity;

1. Knowing that you can meet every need that comes up - there are always enough resources to meet current needs. The fallacy is when we look at a need and believe there is no provision. In

America, we waste a ton of food each day. People eat at a restaurant and leave plenty of food on their plate. It's amazing how those who have resources tend to waste more than those who don't.

2. Knowing that you have more than you will ever need at your disposal - an abundance mentality is necessary to walk in financial prosperity. This mentality will create within us the assurance that we have all that we need whenever we need it. All we have to do is learn how to tap into this abundance, which is all around us.

3. Never think you are lacking anything but think only in abundance - it is very hard to believe "I have abundant resources at my disposal." That is exactly what we must think to achieve our goals. As a man thinks, so shall he become? We have to think that we can meet every need for every occasion if we hope to live that way.

4. Never speak about what you lack, always speak about what you have in abundance - Negative talk does not give us positive results. What you want to see happen in your life you must be willing to say it. The focus has to be on becoming what we envision and that includes being bold enough to say what we mean.

There are many ways to go about creating prosperity. All these various methods do have one concept that ties them all together, though, which is that you need to develop a consciousness of prosperity.

You must have the proper thinking process in place as you go about creating prosperity. This way of thinking is one where you go out of your way to avoid paying interest charges. You will save first and buy the big TV second. When you do buy that TV, it will be with cash you've saved to avoid financing it. The cash you use for your TV will be more than your emergency fund and retirement savings.

Do you see how this financial prosperity mindset is quite different from the mindset of most people you know who are constantly struggling to get out of debt? Do you see how different it is than the mindset they try to sell you on TV or in other various forms of advertising?

Is this harder to do than to just go crazy charging up credit cards and department store accounts like most people? Yes, it is. But, if you desire to attain financial prosperity to live a life of financial success, it's necessary to live by this prosperity consciousness.

That being said, you may be wondering what activities you should be utilizing to attain true financial prosperity. You could do one or more of the following: invest in rental real estate properties, invest into retirement accounts such as IRA's, Roth IRA's, 401(k)'s, Self Employed IRA's, etc., invest in stocks and bonds, invest in option trading, invest in businesses, invest into an emergency account until you have 3 to 6 to 12 months income saved, start a home business (website, network marketing, etc.).

Now, not all of these activities are right for everyone. Some of them require proper training and knowledge to do well.

However, if you're not willing to invest time and energy into learning the specifics of some of these activities that help create prosperity for you, as well as helping when it comes to getting out of debt, financial abundance will elude you.

What if you possess the prosperity consciousness already discussed but lack the financial resources to build that emergency fund or contribute toward that Roth IRA?

If you're serious about financial prosperity, then you may want to see what you can do to increase your income. You've got to fight to find a way to do this. Maybe you need to take a second job to find the seed money for your home business.

You may be closer to creating prosperity than you think. Nowadays, you could set up a simple website that centers on a talent or passion that you have. Rather than thousands, the money needed to get a website started is only a few hundred dollars.

Creating financial prosperity just takes the right mindset, a prosperity consciousness, and the patience to watch your wealth slowly grow.

You'll realize financial abundance once you've worked toward your plan for some years.

CHAPTER 2

BONDAGE OF DEBT

Debts, oh debts. These things are more than enough to drive a person crazy! If you are like most people today, you probably have a debt or two on your back. No problem about that as long as the debt was for something important and that you can make faithful repayments.

However, the situation becomes problematic and stressful when debts start to reach up to your eyeball. When this happens, you would probably start wondering where all these debts came from. The thing is you should not wait until you are deep in debt before you start wondering about this. In fact, it is important that you know the common causes of debts so that you can do your best to avoid them at all cost. Here are the top five most common causes of debts that you should know about.

1. Credit Cards

Credit cards are notorious for tempting people to spend beyond what they can afford. Many people are not aware of the various pitfalls that come with using credit cards for daily expenses. It is even worse when you use it for your impulse shopping sprees. Avoiding using credit cards is one of the best ways to keep you debt and stress-free.

2. Poor Financial Management

Some people just do not realize the importance of proper financial budgeting and expenses recording. A monthly budget is necessary so you can allocate wisely your income among the essential expenditures such as grocery, bills, rent, and so on. Daily recording of expenses, meanwhile, is crucial, so you know where your money is going. Debts can result when you spend beyond your income and you make hundreds of dollars of unnecessary expenses, both of which can be avoided with proper financial planning.

3. Unemployment

Loss of job means no more money is coming in for the household. This would not be a problem if expenses would stop as well, but they don't. Many people who become unemployed resort to using credit cards for their daily expenses even though they are not sure they are capable of repaying these debts.

When all they can afford to pay is the minimum or when they miss monthly payments, the principal debt just grows bigger and bigger. Debts due to unemployment could be avoided if you can save for the rainy day. But if you did not, your best move is to get a new job, fast!

And of course, you should also learn to tone down on your extravagant lifestyle.

4. Gambling

Gambling is one of the most addictive forms of entertainment. Some people end up using the money they don't even have just to keep on playing. This results in piles of debts and loads of stress and anxiety.

5. Little or No Savings

If you have sufficient savings, a job layoff, medical problem, illness, or divorce will not cause havoc in your finances. Not only do you need to start saving, but you should also stop spending tomorrow's money. Even if you are so sure about that job bonus or that monetary gift from your aunt, it is never wise to spend money that is not in your hands yet.

If you are already deep in debt, you can make use of financial strategies that can help alleviate your situation. For example, you can make use of debt consolidation loans such as credit card debt consolidation loan or bad credit consolidation loans, among others. Most of these financial schemes are available from banks, lenders, non-profit debt consolidation services, and credit unions. But if not, it is best to keep yourself debt-free at all times.

6. Living beyond your means:

As we currently live in a 'got to have it now' culture, people can be easily tempted to overspend, by getting something new as soon as it becomes available, whether it's a new car, gadget or fashion fad that has just hit the shelves. Whether it's one big, costly item (e.g. a brand new motor) or lots of less expensive ones (e.g. various bits of new technology), it can all add up, and if someone cannot afford it without the help of credit then they shouldn't really be thinking of getting it in the first place.

7. Redundancy

In the current economic climate, in particular, some people have been affected by redundancies, either directly (themselves) or indirectly (a family member), some who might have been relying on credit as well as their salary to make purchases. If not affected by redundancy, others have seen their hours cut - along with their salary - and bonuses reduced. It's even worse when a family business is affected, or in instances where many members of a family working for the same business are all affected together.

8. A growing family

Whether it's planned or a surprise welcome, the pitter-patter of tiny feet can also result in the cha-ching of not-so-tiny expenses. Baby products can be very expensive, and if financial planning before the arrival has not been thought out properly, the parents-to-be might find that they have to buy more for the infant than previously anticipated, which can lead to the need to borrow money. On top of that, maternity and paternity leave will also affect income - in the form of lower salaries - when taken out.

9. Divorce and separation

If the divorce wasn't expensive enough as it is, with the costly solicitor and legal fees involved, one person's debt could be split amongst both parties, just in the same way that assets are split. In any case, if one of the two people involved remains living in the same house as before, they may find it a lot more difficult on their salary to keep up with payments and expenses that the two of them might have paid together previously.

10. Loss of income:

This is probably the main cause of debt for most people. You can literally have a stable job with a good steady income today, and tomorrow you find yourself drowning in debt. Sometimes, the loss of second income could also be responsible for such a problem because the family has been accustomed to a particular lifestyle and can't go backward. While there is no straight solution to this problem, your only way to avoiding it as much as you can is by being very flexible and patient.

11. Ignorance

Ignorance also plays a major role in getting into debt. Many people throw their money away on everything they stumble on and then complain about the fact that they can't pay their bills. Managing your spending is necessary even if you have an unlimited income. You need to see where your money is going to be able to cut off your unnecessary spending if you needed to

12. No tracking

It's true that people get into debt because of miscalculations they do, but I can assure you that these miscalculations come all from not writing down your numbers. People usually ignore minor spending and not record them because they think that it's unnecessary and that it won't affect their income a lot. However, these minor spending's are usually the ones responsible for major debts.

13. Health

One of the major causes of people getting into debt is that they sometimes get sick and spend all their savings on treatments. If the health condition is a little hard to treat or requires a lot of following, then it's going to be hard not to get into debt that way. There is no solution to this as well unless you have savings to cover your treatments.

CHAPTER 3

BUDGETING

The importance of budgeting for every financial plan is not a subject for debate. If you want to have a successful financial plan, then an effective budgeting strategy is more than necessary. Whether if you are earning six-figures a year or someone who is living from paycheck to paycheck, it is still necessary that you know where you can allocate your financial resources if you want to take control of your finances. Many people are still apprehensive when it comes to the idea of budgeting because they are thinking that budgeting puts restrictions into how and where do they get to spend their money and taking out all the fun in life. But that is not the case at all; budgeting is all about having a sound financial plan so you can have control as to where your money goes and planning the best way to spend that money.

At first, creating a budget may seem to be a huge chore, especially if you are pretty satisfied with how you deal with your finances. But if you just take time to create a budget plan, you will be pleasantly surprised at just how valuable it can be. Through budgeting, you will be able to accurately keep track as to where you are spending your money. This way if you have a certain financial goal in mind, you will be able to accurately gauge just how close you are to reaching your goals, and thus you can take the proper course of action with regards to this matter.

Creating an effective budget plan is not that hard at all, but the tricky part comes into adhering to what sort of budget plan that you have created. To be able to maintain your budgeting plans, you need to approach it with a positive attitude. There's very little success to expect when you think of budgeting as a tedious activity or that you are making a huge sacrifice while doing it. If you want to be able to keep up with your budgeting plan you should think of all the positive effects that you could achieve. Like freedom from debt, save money for recreation or more savings for your retirement plans. You need to keep in mind your goals to keep yourself motivated.

Another thing that you need to keep in mind when maintaining a budget plan is to have realistic expectations. Avoid setting your expectations or goals too high because it can easily discourage you if you fail to fulfill them, and this is especially true when you have just started with your budget plan. If you are just starting with your budget plan, set a realistic yet fairly challenging goal and see if you can keep up with it or not. You can set your goal a little higher next time if you feel confident about it.

Being able to maintain your budget plans and accomplishing your goals is highly rewarding. So if you can keep yourself motivated to fulfill your goals, then you are on your way to budgeting success.

Early Budgeting

Some people don't realize the importance of budgeting and the benefits it can give to you. Budgeting early is not an easy thing to do because it can be easy to lose control of your money. College is the best time to start budgeting your finances. You may have to experiment first on which plan works best for you but of course, like anything else discipline is very important.

But what if I do not have enough money? Well, the more reason for you to start saving up. Start early investing will make a big difference when you start to have more financial activity. The more time you wait, the more complex your financial life will become and the more difficult it will be to stay on a budget. Most college students have average expenses but for others, their expenses are huge and they can hardly control their spending.

Making a budget is somewhat like a goal. If you get to follow it, you will progress financially along with it. Your goal does not necessarily have to be a retirement plan because small plans are as important as the big ones. What matters most is that you get to finish it. If you are still in college, you can start saving up little by little every month or make it a goal to save enough money that you think will cover you for the next month. These small plans may soon lead to larger ones such as student loans.

A good way to start is by keeping track of all your transactions in your account. Knowing how much you spend on your rent or how much is left of you at the end of every month should be considered. Make a budget of your priorities and keep track of it every month to give you a good idea of how much you spend and how much you can save every for each category. This may help you realize if you're spending too much on eating out etc. Determine which categories you should reduce your spending and which ones you should save more. Always keep an eye out for your loans and debts too, make sure you pay them all on time. Create and strategize a plan on how you will pay your debts and keep your credit score report healthy as well.

Budgeting will not only help you manage your finances, but it can improve your credit score as well, which is a good thing for your credit and your future. Regular and on-time payments are the best things you can do to improve your credit score. Get your free credit score from the three credit agencies every year to keep track of it. Let your credit's health services as another reason for you to start budgeting.

Take control of your financial future now. Budgeting will come in handy when you need the money the most.

Personal and Family Budget

A budget is a list of expenses and income. It is the amounts of money that currently comes in and out each month/year. It is also the projected in and out amounts of each month/year.

Displaying anticipated income and expenses allows for a prioritization of expenses, like making mortgage or loan payments before spending money on entertainment and travel. A projected budget provides a framework for making decisions about expenses, such as canceling premium cable services or to saving money for a new automobile. A budget allows you to monitor how close you are to your goals. This knowledge can help you to create budget plans that connect with your daily habits.

Household budget plays a very significant part in the financial security of your family and its financial future. When you have a family, budgeting is certainly becoming harder. I said this because, if you were single, you had to make plans and budgets only for your finance. But once you have a family, you will find it difficult to make financial budgets.

In a family, a new term called 'Family Budget' or 'Household Budget' emerges. In a family, neither the husband nor the wife makes personal budgets. This is not possible. In a family, there are much more expenses than we expect when we are living alone.

When we are alone, we could have spent money on what we wanted and would have been more relaxed. But in a family, you have more family essentials to be purchased like a house, a family car, education of your kids, etc. This becomes more difficult. So, no effective financial planning is possible without a proper and well-defined family budget. This budget now has to include the total family income, the total family expenditure, and the family savings.

It has to be a budget that is shared by all the members of the family. So, it is very clear that the maintaining family finance is an even more difficult job. Hence it is always advisable to make a very well laid family budget that has all the minute financial details. Above all this, remember that the husband and the wife will have to work very hard together to make their financial budgeting a success.

CHAPTER 4

THE HABIT OF SAVING

There are several habits that when once develop, saving becomes your culture.

1. Decide To Save - decide to start saving money. The basic rule is 10% of your income. Get a bookkeeper or personal financial software and start tracking your expenses. Find out where your money is going. Your home-based business has tax advantages that can help you save more.

2. Make your savings an expense - Pay yourself first. Treat your savings like your car note, credit card bill, or mortgage payment. Most people cringe when bill collectors call. Use that same fear to save. Have automatic deductions from your checking account, paycheck, or merchant account go right into your savings. Just like taxes are taking out of a paycheck and most people don't notice it. You won't notice the automatic deductions.

3. Read for 15-30 minutes per day - Your home-based business depends on you. Leaders are readers. Read books on personal finance, money management, investing, and personal development. Start with the Richest Man in Babylon, by George Clauson, followed by Think and Grow Rich, by Napoleon Hill.

4. Pay off your debts - Some experts say that you should pay off your debts first. From my experience, I say to do both. I remember paying off all my debts and still did not have money saved. When I went back into debt when unexpected expenses arrived. Put a portion of your income into savings and a portion of the debt.

Develop a habit of saving money now. Your home-based business depends on it. A habit of saving money is the best way to take care of emergencies, unexpected expenses, and it gives you the ability to act when business opportunities arrive.

Cultivating Saving Habit

Saving money is the art of setting aside some amount of money for future use. The singular reason why so many people don't always get enough money to do what they want or need is that they don't have a good saving habit. In this section, you will learn 6 effective ways to help you start saving money.

1. Determine what you want:

It is very important that you determine what you want to do with money and the time when you would want to use it. Doing this will help ascertain what you should set aside and over what period, for instance, if you desire to save $5,000 within six months, you should be saving about $830 every month. This amount can also be broken down into weeks or days depending on your convenience. What matters most is to ensure that you have a time frame for which to accomplish your goal.

2. Map Out a Plan:

Having established what you want to do with the money you intend to save and over a period, your next task will be to come up with a plan of how you intend to go about the saving. Your plan should entail where to save the money, do you need interests, how often you should save, etc. Planning will help you reach your goal much easier and it will take care of any unforeseen hitches on the way.

3. Discipline:

One of the major reason why lots of people fail to cultivate the habit of saving money is that they lack the discipline required to effective pull through with the plan of saving. Discipline helps you stay focused and committed to your plan. Once you have a plan in place to save some money over a period, you need the discipline to see you through it. Some distractions may come up along the way, but discipline will enable you to pull through.

4. Sacrifice:

Saving demands that you forgo some regular spending routine, the truth is that once you have made up your mind to start saving some money, you will have to make some sacrifices to provide for your savings. By sacrificing some leisure, it means you are making some money available to save. In this case, you will have to differentiate between your needs and wants. One of the best ways to save money is to avoid spending on things you don't need. Besides, when you sacrifice, you should also have it at the back of your mind that it is a temporal basis. That is why it is important that you have a time frame for your saving.

5. Carry Everyone Along:

In the course of saving money, there are so many things that will change with you, especially if you have a family or dependent. In this case, you should endeavor to carry your family and any other person who depends on you financially along. You should be able to communicate your goal to them, am sure if you are convincing enough, they will reason with you.

Saving money is the most effective way to become wealthy in life, no wonder only those who cultivate the habit of saving money can survive in today's economy.

Reasons for Saving

Do you remember the old saying "save for the rainy day"? Can you recall the fable of the ant and the grasshopper we learned when we were young which taught us to save money? Of course, we remember those lessons, yet we don't practice them. It is true that saving money is the greatest secret to building wealth. For you to meet financial security and financial freedom, you need to have a good amount of savings. You are lucky if you are part of the rich clans and have a huge inheritance from your parents' wealth. But what if your parents decided to give it all to charities? Then you're left with nothing. Whether you wanted to become rich or not, you still need to save money.

Here are four important reasons why you still need to save money no matter what:

1. Survive financial crises. This is in the form of accident, illness, job loss, failure of a business, or sudden death either you or one of your family members. Whether this is an act of God or act of nature, there are huge financial losses and we need money to survive. We may find a short-term solution to these problems, but we might end up having huge sums of debts. Adequate savings will give you peace of mind that you can survive any emergency that comes your way.

2. Improve the life and well being of your family. They said that money cannot buy happiness, but it can certainly buy things that will uplift our quality of life and our families. Sufficient savings can help us buy a decent house, a car, pay for quality education or to startup a business. It can also give simple pleasures for

your love ones like treating them to vacations or trips. It can also strengthen married life. Most couples argue about the lack of money. With enough savings, we can avoid disagreements about finances.

3. Enjoy your retirement.

4. Economic development.

Whether you wanted to become rich or not, you still need to save money. Believe it or not, money makes the world go round. Money is essential for survival, and in this world and age, things are no longer free. To secure your future, you need to save money and start early so you can enjoy its fruits sooner.

CHAPTER 5

CREDIT CARDS

Financial problems are something most of us will have to manage eventually in life. With the economic difficulties, we are enduring as a globe presently means that for most of us, "sooner" is now.

Financial struggles and their resulting impact on person's credit are quite regular topics of conversations whether you are personally involved in discussing such details yourself, or you are overhearing others trying to brainstorm what to do next to recover from money problems.

As our economy begins to recover and grow again, so will the financial health of individuals, begin to be able to turn the focus of finances on recovery instead of mere survival. However, as we are starting to turn that corner and have the luxury of having enough income to be able to spare energy and thought in the direction of fixing the damage that has been done to our credit histories. This leaves the field wide open for scammers and unsavory individuals to attempt to take advantage of the situation.

Once our finances have revived to the point of being able to be concerned with more than just having a roof over our heads and food in our cabinet, thoughts invariably, turn to asking, what to do next.

Financially you "bite the dust". Thus, you will find yourself trying to figure out how to dust off your credit. This will eventually, have you looking for ways to repair it to a point of being a tool for improving your life and reaching life goals instead of holding you back from accomplishing what you want to do with the rest of your life.

The question now becomes how to repair your credit.

How can you repair your credit? How do you fix the damage that has been done by financial difficulties and later move on? Is fixing your credit something you consider impossible to do on your own?

The reality is you can learn how to repair your credit and safeguard your finances on your own without needing to pay someone else to do it for you. Actually, it is far better for both your present and your future if you learn how to take care of, maintain, and monitor your financial health status for yourself, as no one will consider your finances to be more important than you will.

So take that strong motivation inside of you that causes you to want to control your own destiny as much as possible, and consider the suggestions that follow as stepping stones guiding your steps to credit repair and eventual financial freedom.

Defining and understanding credit

This chapter will explain what credit is; discuss the benefits of credit to consumers and our economy at large.

Credit can be defined as an item of value that is given to another for care, protection or performance. The concept behind credit is, "Receive now and pay later." When an applicant is approved for a credit card, the issuing company is entrusting the card, with its available purchasing power, to a consumer. As opposed to issuing the card for care and protection, the merchant's primary motive for extending credit is performance and, of course, to make a profit.

In this context, performing would consist of a consumer using the credit card to make purchases. This is what the card issuer wants consumers to do. The idea of "receiving now and paying later" allows most people to enjoy luxuries of a higher standard of living. How many of us would be able to visit the local Lexus dealer and pay for a new car with spot cash? Not many, I gather. Credit allows us to protract our repayment obligation over a period (sometimes defined and other times not), thereby alleviating the burden of responsibility of an immediate debt.

Credit allows us the comfort and convenience of shopping online, via telephone, through catalogs and so on. In fact, in some areas, individuals cannot even receive movie rental memberships without guaranteeing them with a credit card. Rental cars and vehicles used to aid in moving must also be reserved for credit or debit cards. In this light, credit offers consumers a variety of products and services that would otherwise be inaccessible or at least difficult to enjoy.

Banks and various loan institutions also benefit from the use of credit. While they may not require full payment of debt up front, they earn money from finance charges, over-the-limit fees, late fees (which have gradually increased over time) and other expenses that they impose.

Upon accepting a loan, a consumer is agreeing to repay a bank for not only the original amount of the loan but also any finance charges that may have been assessed based on his or her credit history and other factors. Financing of most loans is fixed, meaning that it cannot change unless the debt is refinanced.

Credit cards, however, work a bit differently. The annual percentage rates may vary based on various factors, such as the end of a promotion, occurrence of a late payment made by a cardholder, adverse or positive review of a cardholder's credit history by issuing company and so forth.

Some of these factors could result in a consumer receiving a more competitive annual percentage rate than he or she previously had. For example, sometimes we receive letters from our existing banks or credit card providers informing us that they have increased our credit limits due to good payment history. Be wary: a higher credit limit sounds tantalizing, but its primary purpose is to heighten your debt.

Higher credit limits equal higher risks for most consumers. What they do not mention is that they have also reviewed our credit records. This is legal. When we enter into contracts with issuers of credit (meaning, we accept the card), we are giving them the authorization to review our credit histories as often as they would like during the life of the account. However, do not be alarmed! These types of credit reviews (frequently referred to as "soft inquiries") are not detrimental to your overall credit rating. On the other hand, if a bank assesses an adverse review of your credit, you may receive a letter advising that your annual percentage rate has increased, your credit limit has been decreased, or even worse, your account has been closed. Consumers must always read the fine print on all credit applications for loans and cards.

Most consumers regard credit as an intricate and confusing concept. This approach is taken because people fear the unknown. Enlightened, educated and well-informed consumers understand how credit works and the importance of it. By understanding credit and viewing it in a mutualistic manner, it is not such a bad concept after all. Credit offers both merchants and consumers a variety of benefits.

Establishing Credit and Responsibility

No credit

One of the most commonly asked questions by consumers is, "How do I establish credit if I keep getting denied credit?" The truth is, building credit for the first time can be accomplished in some ways. If a person has attempted to create credit for the first time and has been denied, it is not a good idea to continue applying for credit with various companies. If this pattern of behavior is maintained, it will only result in a credit record overflowing with creditor inquiries. This chapter will give you insight into establishing credit for the first time, as well as tell you how to go about reestablishing credit after a financial setback has occurred.

One significant way to build credit is to ask a friend or relative with good credit history to co-sign for or with you on an application. When this happens, the person who already has credit established will share responsibility in some capacity for making sure the account remains in good standing and is paid promptly.

The other party's relationship with the account will vary, depending upon whether the account is established as joint/shared or co-sign/co-maker. Joint/Shared means both parties share equal responsibility for repayment of the debt associated with the account. Cosigner/co-maker indicates that one party is primarily responsible for payment (this person is referred to as the "maker" or "primary") however, the other party agrees to assume complete responsibility if the first borrower defaults.

Regardless of your role in the process, it is important to know that your credit history will reflect the other party's payment pattern on the associated account. This means, if one party defaults and becomes delinquent on the debt, the negative rating related to the late(s) will also be submitted to your credit record.

Some financial advisors have misled consumers into thinking they can obtain another person's credit score by becoming an authorized user on a credit card. This information is simply not right. We'll discuss this more in the credit-scoring chapter. But keep in mind that it is wise to exercise extreme caution anytime you may be considering entering into a loan contract with another party, regardless of who the other person is.

Many times consumers experience adverse credit ratings at the hands of the ones closest to them, including relatives and loved ones. Be careful! If you are not able to persuade a friend or about cosign for you, try asking him or her to add you to an existing revolving account as an authorized user. This method is often the preferred method because you may enjoy all of the benefits of having a charge card, with minimal responsibility. If you are an authorized user on the account, it means you can charge and make purchases but are not directly responsible for making the payment to the creditor. The account will also be reported to your credit record, listing you as a user.

If you choose to become an authorized user, you must understand that if the person responsible for making the loan payment defaults, the negative rating will also be reported to your credit history. This technique is still one of choice, however, because even if the negative rating gets attached to your credit record, if you contest the item through the credit-reporting company, most of the time the creditor will expunge the entry from your history because you were only listed as an authorized user. Just know the risk involved in becoming an authorized user. (In this scenario, it is also a good idea to contact the creditor directly and request that the account is removed from your credit record. You may have to submit such an application in writing, but it is worth the time and energy if you can get the negative entry removed from your credit report.)

Three basic types of credit

There are three fundamental types of credit accounts: open, installment and revolving. Let's spend some time discussing each of them.

Open accounts are accounts that require full payment for services received at the end of each billing cycle. These types of accounts will never request a minimum payment. Examples of open accounts include:

- Gas cards (such as Shell, Amoco).

- Utility accounts (telephone, gas, electricity).

- Cellular accounts (Verizon and Nextel, for example)

Installment accounts are ones that have a fixed monthly repayment amount. The amount of the payment can only change if the debt has been refinanced. Examples of installment accounts are:

- Student loans.

- Auto loans.

- Personal loans.

- Mortgage loans.

- Recreational merchandise loans (boats, motorcycles, and so on)

Revolving accounts require a minimum payment of a larger existing balance at the end of the monthly billing cycle. They do not require full payment of a balance owed at the end of each billing period, however, any unpaid amount that carries over is subject to additional charges. Revolving accounts include, for instance, Credit cards (such as Visa and MasterCard). Department store/retail cards (such as Sears, JC Penney, Macy's, Best Buy and Circuit City)

Revolving accounts are often accused of being the inducers of bad credit. The truth is that credit cards must be used wisely and when they are, can have very effective bargaining power. Basic advice is to never charge an amount on a credit card that exceeds your ability to repay it in full within 30 days. This is the golden rule! If the amount is repaid in full at the end of the billing cycle, no additional charges will be assessed. This is often where creditors "trick us," so to speak. They offer a minimum amount due, but subsequently; attach charges to the remaining unpaid balance that carries over to the next billing period. This technique, along with late fees, annual membership fees, and so on, is what allows them to make profits from consumers.

Dealing with Credit Challenges During a Recession

Whether you're in a committed relationship or married, with or without kids, the chances are likely that demands on your time are greater than ever. Not that you need a recap, but let's examine some of the challenges you may be experiencing or observing weekly if not daily:

- Your employer is demanding more productivity from each employee, and that translates into longer hours, tighter deadlines and more overall pressure on you at work.

- Because banks have been nervous about their balance sheets, you may have had some of your credit lines frozen, or cut, reducing your family's ability to access financing without applying for new credit cards.

- You want to take buy a house because of the low prices in the current real estate market, but higher credit score requirements have you temporarily 'locked out' as a potential buyer. You have excellent credit scores, but being self-employed, you take every tax write-off available, and cannot document enough net income to qualify for a mortgage without a 30%-40% down payment (Currently 23% - 25% of potential homebuyers in the U.S.).

- Mortgage interest rates are the lowest they have been in over 50 years, but you cannot qualify to refinance your home because your credit scores are too low and/, or you don't have enough equity. Each one of the external factors listed above is another variable that can further complicate your life, and many of the examples are completely out of your control. This doesn't include the fact that if you have children, the responsibilities you need to juggle feels like each child multiplies them.

However, we are here to let you know that regardless of what's going on in the world around you, you still have the ability to navigate your family's finances through the morass. As you may already know, the more external variables/factors that you need to manage, the more challenging it is to feel like you have some control of your life. The best way to offset this dynamic is to maximize every factor YOU can control by increasing the depth and breadth of your knowledge, understanding, and experience, while increasing your efforts through self-discipline, continuous learning, and hard work.

CHAPTER 6

UNDERSTANDING CREDIT REPORTS

The written report that lenders depend on is called your credit report. A credit report is essentially a history of your entire financial life, from your first credit card to the present time. Three major companies track your credit. They are called credit bureaus. These companies— Equifax, Transunion, and Experian—all keep similar records of your credit history. When a lender is considering giving you a loan or a credit card, the lender will contact one of the three credit bureaus for a copy of your credit history. By the information in your file, the lender will decide whether to take a risk with you, how much to lend you, and at what interest rate.

When you hear credit reports being discussed, usually you will hear them referred to as "snapshots" of individual finances. While that may be technically accurate to a point, it is also rather misleading because credit reports usually contain far more information about your financial life than what the word "snapshot" portrays.

If you have been, an adult and running your finances, your credit report will be more than just a page or "snapshot". In fact, unless you have kept your personal finances separate from any banks or financial institutions and paid for everything in cash, your credit report will have at least 5-10 pages of unique information about your finances.

The longer you spend money and interact with financial institutions, the longer your credit report will be. However, a lengthy credit report is not necessarily a bad thing – it is only "bad" for you if it is showing serious money mismanagement, overwhelming debt, and unreliability regarding repayment of debts. Even then, it is not really a "bad" thing either – it is simply made up of your facts, your financial actions, and your financial history.

As the proverb goes, "knowledge is power" and that is never truer than when it comes to your personal finances. In addition, credit reports will contain the most relevant financial information that you need no matter what season of life you are currently in.

Your unique credit report usually will give you one of three overall messages:

1. Your finances are a mess, you are in deep debt, and it is time to pick up the reigns again to your finances and take control before it's too late, financially speaking, or

2. Your finances are well in-hand, you clearly have control over your income and outflow, and you exert that control in

financially responsible ways for the good of yourself and your loved ones, or

3. You have (or have not) made any progress regaining control over your finances since the last time you read your credit report.

Sections of credit reports

Credit reports have six main sections that are personalized with your specific numbers to show you not only where your finances are today, but also shows improvements (or lack thereof) which let you know where you need to focus to see faster progress regarding debt reduction or financial security.

Personal Information

The first section contains your personal information that goes far beyond your name and mailing address. Of course, it has the identifying information needed. Also it also your legal name (or names if you have legally changed your name at any time), your birth year, all addresses on record for your past and present, and also all of the places you have been legally employed since your very first day in the official workforce in any arena.

While most understand how important it is to protect identifying information such as social security number, bank account numbers, etc., other details are often overlooked concerning protection.

Those looking to steal identities can use seemingly unimportant facts about our lives that might seem irrelevant to identity theft such as prior addresses and employer history. Some of those details can be found through internet searches, but it is important to be mindful that those facts can be used in conjunction with other details to steal or damage your credit reputation.

Summary

The summary of your personal credit is usually found within the first couple of pages of your credit report and often includes the following information:

- How many accounts listed negatively?

- How many accounts in collections.

- Total amount of real estate debt (home or properties)

- Total amount of debts considered installment loans (car loans, appliance loans, etc.).

- Total amount of revolving debt (a.k.a. credit cards)

- Percentage of revolving credit available

Credit History & Debt

This section has the primary information for your credit report and contains the most important information from both your perspective and anyone else's perspective that has reason to be scrutinizing your credit.

It is a list of all of your credit accounts – ones currently open, but also ones that have been closed. This is also, where the same creditors will indicate problems with late or missing payments. With all that significant and personal information, it is critical for you to look very carefully through the details each time you run your report.

If you find any errors in the numbers, or there are credit accounts you do not recognize as belonging to you, you need to send a dispute letter immediately to the credit agency who generated the report as well as to the company, which had added incorrect information to your report.

For each creditor/account on your report, you should be able to see the following specifics documented:

Creditor Information – name of the company reporting information about your account

Your Account Number – unique to the company

Responsible Parties – the name or names of the people responsible for the account, usually using one or more abbreviations:

I – Individual

U – Undesignated

J – Joint

A - Authorized User

M – Maker

T – Terminated

C - Co-maker/Co-signer

S – Shared

Opening Date – the month and year the account was opened with the creditor.

Creditor Reporting – how many months the creditor has been reporting information concerning the account.

Last Account Activity – the date of the last activity of any kind by anyone on the account.

Understanding credit scores

Once one has his/her credit report which determines the credit score, one is in a position to tell they stand and also one can tell where exactly many of their problems lie. In case of a poor score, from your credit report one should try to figure out what could be the cause of the problem:

- Find out if you may be having too much debt?

- Too many bills that are not paid?

- Have you faced any major financial upset recently?

- Have you by any chance not had credit long enough to establish for you a good credit?

- Have you defaulted any a loan, not paid taxes, or you may have been reported or not been cleared by a collection agency?

First off, there are certain factors that are not part of your credit score calculation. They include your employment information, occupation, salary, race, color, sex, marital status plus much more. Keep in mind that the only thing that goes into the calculation of your score is actual credit information.

What Affects My Credit Score?

Your credit score is a snapshot or a brief of your credit profile at that moment in time. The credit factors that go into calculating your score are amounts owed, payment history, and the length of credit history, types of credit used and new credit.

Payment History

This is obvious, but payment history makes up about 35% of your score. Missing a payment has a huge impact on your credit score, so it is crucial to pay all credit accounts on time. If you are currently late on any debts, you want to get those accounts current as soon as possible. The credit bureaus give the highest weight to payment history over the last 24 months.

Amounts Owed

There are many people who pay their debts on time and still have a low score because they have high balances on credit accounts like a credit card. The balances on accounts make up about 30% of your credit score. To increase your score, you want to pay down on your credit card accounts and maintain the balances as low as possible.

Length of Credit History

The length of credit refers to how long an account has been open. The longer the account has been open, the higher your score will be. Credit history makes up about 15% of your score. This is why it is so important to not close out any accounts as this could lower your score, even if you never use the account. By closing out the account, you will lose the history of that account when it comes to calculating your credit score.

New Credit

Anytime you open a new account, your score will drop until the account begins to have some credit history. New accounts only make up about 10% of your score, so you will not see a large drop in your score on a new account, but opening several accounts at one time will greatly affect your score. You should only open a new account if you need too.

Types of Credit Used

It is crucial to have good credit accounts on your report. Avoid finance company loans or accounts that have 90 days. Installment loans, Mortgage loans, and revolving credit cards impact your credit score much more favorably compared to the finance company accounts. This makes up about 10% of your credit score.

Improving Your Credit Score

This discussion will focus on improving your credit scores and provide you with information on how you can do even more to improve your credit status. Doing so will go a long way towards improving your credit score because your credit score is derived from the information in the credit report. But there is, even more, you can do.

This chapter covers techniques for raising your credit score as high as possible. The benefits will be two-fold—you will have greater access to credit and the credit you obtain will cost less.

What You Need To Know!

You may find that your credit score is still lower than you would like (or deserve) even after making sure your credit report is accurate. The average FICO credit score has fluctuated between 675 and 700 in recent years, with 850 being the maximum score one could have. People with below average scores must pay high- interest rates.

What Can You Do?

First, you need to recognize that efforts to improve your credit score take time to have an impact. Most people find that it takes about one year for their score to show much improvement. This is partly because changes take time to show up in your credit report.

But it is also true that your credit history stays with you for a long time. If your history is positive, that is a real plus. But if your history has some negatives, those stay in your credit file for six-seven years. New positive information helps, but it does not erase old negative information.

Nonetheless, waiting to do something about a low score only prolongs the problem. The time to get started is now. Basically, there are two broad categories of the things you can do to improve your credit score. The first involves improving your financial behaviors. The second involves changing your debt situation. For each, let's list things you should DO and things you should NOT DO.

Improving Your Financial Behaviors

DO pay your bills on time. The largest single component of a credit score is your payment history. If you are late on or skip payments on items such as credit cards or vehicle loans, your score will surely be affected. This is true for installment debt payments—such as a television—and any of your monthly bills, such as your utilities. This is because of many merchants—not just lenders—report a payment pattern to credit bureaus.

DO focus any search to obtain new credit within a short period of time, such as one month. The number of inquiries from lenders in your credit bureau file has a negative effect on your credit score. If the inquiries all come in within thirty days they will all be recognized as part of one search—such as for an auto loan. But if you spread your search over several months the pattern will look like multiple searches— negative in most credit scoring systems.

DO check your credit score periodically—perhaps every six months while you are working to rebuild your credit score. Your own inquiries do not negatively impact your credit score. Make sure you get your score directly from the credit bureaus or from FICO. Using the second party to get the score (such as the many "free offers" you might see on the Internet) will be viewed as coming from a lender. This means they will be counted as a lender inquiry, and that is a negative.

DO avoid applying for any new credit for one year. Inquiries from creditors are automatically deleted from your record after twelve months. This technique is especially helpful if your credit report currently shows a high number of inquiries.

DO NOT ignore bills for which you are currently behind. Bring them up-to-date. DO NOT open multiple new accounts just to show a credit history. If you have had little credit in the past, open no more than one or two accounts and build your history slowly.

DO NOT close old accounts. Length of credit history definitely will have a positive impact on your credit score. Having a large number of accounts that are in good standing that have zero balances definitely is a plus, but not a negative.

Changing Your Debt Situation

DO reduce your balances on your credit cards and other loans. If you a high outstanding balance on one or more of your credit cards, you will lose points on your score. Lower balances tend to lead to higher FICO® scores. Pay down your balances and keep them low.

DO NOT open new accounts to transfer high balances and spread your total debt across multiple accounts. If you feel you could benefit by moving a portion of the balance on one card to another, use an existing account. Of course, you would not want to move a balance from a low-interest rate card to one that has a higher rate.

DO get help if you are having trouble paying your debts. It may be possible to have your debts renegotiated if you can show that your difficult financial situation is temporary and it can be improved over time. For example, you may have fallen behind in your bills because of unemployment but you are working again now. You can contact lenders directly or use a reputable not-for-profit credit-counseling agency. You are not asking your creditors for forgiveness here—you are just asking for a little more time.

DO pay off any late or written-off debt. These items will still stay on your credit report but the fact that you made good on the debt will be a plus.

DO re-establish your credit if you have had problems in the past. Opening one or two credit accounts and using them responsibly will slowly but surely rebuild your credit score. This may take a few years, however. DO stop using your credit cards if you are not paying your balance in full each month. Using a card on which you carry a balance is almost guaranteed to result in ever-increasing balances.

DO NOT ignore debt problems. Credit scores can go down much faster than they can go up. Lenders typically report negative information right away. Again, contacting lenders directly or a telephoning a reputable credit-counseling agency can be of help.

DO NOT use repossession as a way to get out from under a debt. Repossession negatively affects credit scores even if the repossessed item has sufficient value to pay the debt. And in most cases, its value is not enough to pay off the full balance owed. Thus you will still owe some amount of remaining debt. It would be better to sell the item yourself, add additional funds if necessary, and pay off the debt in full.

What You Can Do! Action Module: Improving Your Credit Score

Now that you know some of the DO-s and DON'T-s of improving your credit score, it's time to take action. The two worksheets below can help you chart a course towards a better credit score. The first will help you make sure you pay your bills on time. The second provides a checklist of the steps you want to take to build your credit score.

CHAPTER 7

IMPULSE BUYING

Retailers make a fortune each year on consumer's impulse buying and although it is good for them, it can leave a hole in our purse not to mention the clutter that results from impulsive buying. Yes, it makes us feel good when we buy the things that we want as well as the things that we need, but it is important to use wisdom in our spending.

Impulsive buying is an addiction. I know it is true because I was once an impulsive buyer. There is a resale store in my community that I loved to visit and buy from, the prices were low, so I bought whatever I liked whether I needed it or not. I would bring the item or items home and store it away. Well, one day I decided to do some spring-cleaning and I realized that I had five big boxes of stuff that I had purchased from that resale shop. That was when it dawned on me that I was addicted to buying in that store. Of course, I did not buy everything at once, but over the course of time, I had spent a small fortune on things that I was not using. I purposed in my heart that I would stop going there at least for a while, but it was not an easy to do because I craved going shopping there. However, I forced myself to stay away and pretty soon the desire for that place left me.

There are many impulsive buyers without the fortitude within themselves to quit this addiction, but there are things that can be done to lessen the craving and perhaps eventually stop it altogether.

Leave credit or debit cards at home. People who have access to money tend to overspend while shopping.

Make a list of the things that you need and stick to the list.

Stay away from your favorite department. If what you need is not in that department, do not go there to browse. You might end up spending money on something you like instead of on what you need.

Buy only things that you can return, the reason for this is because we buy on impulse and maybe a few days later we might realize that we do not want it, so a return policy is handy in a situation such as that.

Do not be tempted by sale items; you might not need it.

Go shopping alone or at least with someone who budgets well. To shop alone may not be, as much fun so you will leave the store sooner and a person who budgets himself will also keep you on track.

Budget yourself, before you leave home to take with you the amount of money you are willing to spend and do not forget to leave credit cards at home. Once the money that you have with you is done, then you are done.

Do not browse around in the store; this is more temptation to buy and most likely it would be something that you do not need.

Never shop when upset, I have heard people say that shopping takes their mind off their problem, but it can also put a dent in your purse so instead of shopping if you become upset, take a walk. Fresh air will do more for you any day than shopping.

Impulse buying is something that brick and motor & e-commerce shops want us to do. Retail displays are set up to maximize the amount of money we spend and to tempt us into buying more than we intended. Online sites like Amazon do similar things with their recommendations and lists of stuff that other people like you also bought. So how can you stop - or at least cut-down - your impulse buying?

Don't revenge shop

If you're upset with someone or something, comfort shopping is bad for your wallet. Unless you go out without cash or credit cards or ID (just in case the store try to get you to open one of their accounts)

Then window-shopping is possibly OK. But the temptation to go back home and open the nearest Internet browser just to get your impulse buying fix is still way too strong.

Choose your shopping friends wisely

Some friends are good to shop with and will help you to restrain yourself when you are about to impulse buy.

But other friends - you already know the ones - will act like that little devil on your shoulder in movies. They'll encourage you to buy anything and everything in sight and will be on the side of the shop's profits rather than your future credit card bill.

Beware special offers

Every supermarket knows the special offer tricks work. So do most shops except maybe the smallest mom and pop ones.

The offers of two (or even three) for one on something you never planned to buy are designed to get you to open your wallet.

The same goes for extra free items. You get 20% or whatever more of something that was never on your shopping list in the first place.

And reduced prices are the worst. Too often the crossed through price was only ever available in the shop's dreams, waiting for the requisite number of days to pass before the item can be marked down to show you a fantastic saving that gets you back to roughly the correct price in the first place.

Put your inquisitive, questioning, eyes on super sharp mode whenever you see a special offer.

Use "I'll think about it."

This gives you breathing space from the high-pressure sales techniques that pressurize you to into spending on impulse.

The salesman's eyes will show their look of disappointment but don't let that push you into making the purchase.

Go for a walk around the block or - better yet - come back tomorrow if you really must have whatever that special offer is.

It will almost certainly still be there - especially on sneaky Internet sites with countdowns that cunningly re-set every day.

Use a list and a budget

Writing things down on paper may be old fashioned, but that doesn't mean it's not a good way to do things.

Jot down the items you want to buy and your target price range.

Then stick to your guns - if it's not on your list or the price is too high, pluck up the courage to just say "no."

How to Stop Impulse Buying

To be successful financially demands that you get a firm grip on where your money is going. It will be a bad idea to work for a month and spend your income frivolously on items you don't need in the first place. Money is a magnet and it has wings to fly when you mismanage it. Impulse buying is one of the loopholes to watch out for in your finances. It is one of the easiest ways to throw away money on things you don't need. Here are some ways to regain control of your money:

Make a list: If you are going to stop buying on impulse, then you need to have a list handy before you go to that supermarket or shopping mall. A simple list of the items will guide you on what to buy. Advertisements, store displays, and coupons will try to entice and convince you to buy things that aren't on your list. Make sure you use your list to help you resist impulse buying. Stick to the items you have on your list.

Shop when you need something: Shop when you only need something, NOT for fun or to cheer yourself up. That's when you're most prone to impulse buying and bad shopping judgment. Go to the mall with the aim of getting something you desperately need.

Think before you take any action: Before making any purchase or buying decision, leave the store to think it over. If the salesperson has been using pressure tactics, don't go back. Pressure tactics include statements like "It's the last one in stock." "If you buy one right now, I'll give you an additional discount." "This is a once-in-a-lifetime deal."

Seek for alternatives: Is there a less expensive alternative? Is there a supermarket that sells less across the road? Instead of buying one item, can you buy a dozen or half to reduce cost? Frequently, you can save by buying a less-expensive model. You can also buy just about any quality item second-hand. Check the classifieds in your local newspaper, or use the Internet.

Buy, rent or borrow: Consider renting or borrowing instead of buying. For major purchases, such as a snow blower, lawn tractor, etc., ask yourself if you will use it enough to justify owning it. You don't need to buy every item you need because you end up using some items just once.

CHAPTER 8

PRIORITIZE EXPENDITURE

Except for the rich, we all need to watch our spending. Money management is a very simple concept; spend less than we earn! It is easy to say, but difficult to do especially at various stages of our lives.

When we are young we are like a growing business; we need to invest in homes, our families and other things for getting established. This makes it almost impossible to spend less than we earn, so it is necessary to use debt to build our lives. It is also necessary to establish priorities for what we buy with cash or debt.

If we prepare a budget early on it will help us get control of our necessities very quickly. If we are honest, we discover that it doesn't take a lot of income just to survive. Then we need to focus on making enough money to pay for them and have some money left over, or profit as a business would call it. Our profit should be invested in a backup fund and other things we need to build our lives and live free. This is a very over-simplified financial model, but it is a very fundamental one.

Prioritizing our expenditures that are not necessities is where we often get into trouble. Overspending results in high credit card balances that are difficult to be free of and only makes it more difficult for us to invest in the things we want, such as a house and improved living standards.

So, how do we establish priorities on how we use our discretionary cash? There are many resources for guiding us in making these decisions, but I have another way to look at it. We should prioritize our discretionary spending on what will make us happy!

My definition of happiness is to have inner peace, purpose in life and to make a living that gives me financial freedom. If we have credit cards that are overextended, we will worry and have stress that inhibits our inner peace. If we focus too much on just ourselves, we will only see tons of things we want for self-fulfillment. We may also fall into envying others for what they have and seek to get those things for ourselves. We can become greedy, even if we are not wealthy. We often fall into a "pity party" when we get too self-centered and believe we are "victims" as we are not paid enough, and don't have as much money as we deserve. This will only take us down and destroy our inner peace.

If we learn to be thankful for what we have and understand how much others don't have, our attitude can change. We can even consider using some of our discretionary money to help others.

So our spending priorities should be based on a higher level, that of having real happiness; inner peace, purpose, and freedom that comes from controlling our debt. Some would call this avoiding instant gratification; I call it seeking total happiness.

Whenever we spend we should ask ourselves the simple question, would this make us happy?

CHAPTER 9

BEING RICH

A millionaire mindset does not just happen to most. Becoming a millionaire isn't about snapping your fingers and poof you have it. Bank accounts don't just fill because we want them to. There are several traits and steps that must be taken. Here are a few of the traits you need to live your dream with money in your pocket.

A Vision

Having a Millionaire mindset starts with a vision. A millionaire has a creative vision with a positive attitude. This means that not only do millionaires have big dreams but also they truly believe that their dreams will come true and they will do anything they need to see that dream come true. You are what your thoughts are. Setting a large personal goal and seeing it through to fruition is a huge start towards dollars in the pocket.

Thinking Differently

Millionaires don't just think differently about money, but they think differently about everything. While most are spending time on menial, nonproductive tasks, a person with a millionaire mindset is spending brainpower on ways to create their path. Independent thinking doesn't necessarily mean doing the opposite of everyone else; it means finding the courage to follow your dreams even if they don't always conform to everyone else's thinking. Millionaires find ways for money to work for them; they don't chase money. For example, if your dreams are to become a world-renowned author, then focus your thinking on ways to do that.

Having Skills

Millionaires never quit learning new skills. They read, they learn and constantly go with the times. Instead of hanging around with people who have the same skill level as they do, they normally will hang around and choose colleagues who offer a supplement to their weaker skills. So to learn new skills, you can use training or mentors to strengthen your skills. Those with a millionaire mindset will normally choose a mentor that is in a position that they strive to be in. For example, if someone is striving to be a millionaire, they don't hang out or use mentors that aren't making a million dollars already. They don't hang out with people with a job mentality.

Have Passion

The millionaire mindset also has a lot to do with passion. To millionaires, money is just a byproduct of something that they like to do very much. You have to have a true passion for what you are doing to incorporate it into every part of your life. The statistic of finding your true passion isn't until approximately age 45 and achieving the million dollars, or more usually isn't statistically until age 54. If you want to be a millionaire, start doing things that make your heart sing and stop doing things that you do not love. If you are not sure what that is, start trying new things until you find the right fit for you!

Being a Salesman

Those with a millionaire mindset also know that salesmanship is one of the best skills they can learn. Millionaires constantly are presenting their ideas and persuading other people to buy into their visions. That is all sales is; persuasion and getting people to buy in. A good salesperson has a tough diamond skin that is oblivious to naysayers and critical people. Millionaires also have great interpersonal skills and can socialize well. It starts with being able to sell yourself so polish and practice this skill every single day on someone, anyone. It not only helps you get better at the skill of sales but also helps you build a larger, more loyal network of people.

Smart Investing and Living Within Your Means

When you are a millionaire, spending a few hundred bucks on a shopping trip seems like no big deal and it isn't. But while you are trying to get there, you need to mind your dollars and cents. Someone with a millionaire mindset will make sure they are spending smart and spending on the right things. The right things to invest in are yourself, your education you need for your idea, and it never hurts to budget. Would you rather go without that extra latte for a few years if you knew that you could have everything your heart desires?? Of course, you would!

Unfortunately, becoming a millionaire doesn't come at the drop of the hat and is a risk, to say the least, but the advantages far outweigh the disadvantages. With some confidence, the ability to make a strong decision put those new skills to the test and to never let that vision out of your site (not even for a minute); you can have whatever you want in life and your pocket!

Well, creating a millionaire mindset is pivotal to your success in business especially in network marketing. This may be why you are struggling with no success in your business and wondering why. Even if you have the best business opportunity, the best compensation plan, or even the best marketing system, not changing your mindset will have you spinning in circles and not achieving any success. So here are three pivotal pillars to help you in creating a millionaire mindset. They are education, company, and activity.

Education

What do you put into your brain daily? In other to create a millionaire mindset you have to increase your knowledge and the only way of doing this is by educating yourself. There are no shortcuts! You have to invest in educating yourself on the industry of network marketing, as this is the only way you will understand what the business is about. There are a variety of books out there on the industry and mindset some are Think and Grow Rich by Napoleon Hill, Rich Dad Poor Dad by Robert Kiyosaki, How to Win Friends and Influence People by Dale Carnegie and a host more!

Another way of acquiring information is by attending live events and training. This can be powerful; as you do not just get the training you also build relationships with fellow like-minded individuals. Education is critical because we are all a product of what we believe and we tend to believe what we know. So if what you know is not getting you closer to creating a millionaire mindset then I guess you have to improve that by learning new material. You have to know exactly where you want to be and what your goals you want to achieve. In network marketing, you have to believe that you are going to be successful in whatever you are doing.

You must avoid negative thoughts and be positive at all times, thoughts or comments like "I will try" or "I hope this works" automatically sets your brain up for failure. You should be confident that your business would succeed because you will be responsible for making it a success. You are the only one that has the power to make your life the way you want it, and it can be done only if you educate yourself the right way.

Company

A saying goes, "tell me your friends and I will tell you who you are." This rings true for the most part. In creating a millionaire mindset, you have to be in the company of the people you would like to be like. I am not saying to dump your friends/family and make new ones. However, you have to truly evaluate those that encourage you in what you are doing and those that try to pull you down as a result of their lack of understanding. Answer this, "Are you living for your friends and family or you?" For you, I hope!

You should keep your relationships, but focus on associating yourself with the people you want to be like, learn from them, and duplicate their success. A great place to meet people is in training seminars as I mentioned above. Lifelong relationships are built this way. Time is the most important asset in the world and if you waste it associating primarily with the wrong people then creating a millionaire mindset for yourself will never be realized.

Activity

What actions do you take on a daily basis in creating that millionaire mindset? Watch TV? Browse the Internet? To create a millionaire mindset you need to get laser-focused on taking action. You have to develop a plan, goal or a systematic approach to whatever you set out to do. You have to turn your education into action and be consistent with it. In business, the success that everyone wants is not a mystery, but just having the mindset of doing the things that others won't do.

I have often heard that working paycheck to paycheck will never make one a millionaire; this is not consistent in creating a millionaire mindset. According to the late Jim Rohn, "in other to make a fortune you have to make profits" So if you are in this situation, you have thought of doing something else or adding to what you are doing now. You would have to learn how to shift from the employee mentality to the entrepreneur mentality. Yes, granted this is a long potentially difficult process, however, if you do not start it, it will never be done.

Sounds radical? Yes, it is, but if you can wrap the mind around this concept, then you can slowly start changing how you think and start learning new skills. You have to decide to change what you are doing if it is not getting you to creating a millionaire mindset of success.

So there you have it, creating a millionaire mindset is crucial to your success in business. Remember that this is a process. There has to be a mental shift in how you think about your mindset to change.

You may find that they have been working so hard for and don't have any money left over at the end of the month to pay your bills. Possibly you do not have money put away for luxuries like going on a Caribbean cruise or having a luxurious vacation in Seychelles. Are you still driving around in your old banger of a car while all the time someone else is showing off their latest gleaming car to add to their collection?

What is it that she/he has that you don't? Are they just luckier than you are? Probably, the big difference between you and that person is that they have cultivated a millionaire mindset.

You are probably thinking to yourself right now, "what is a millionaire mindset?" Well you see, your mind is very powerful. But do you know that your subconscious mind is even more powerful? The subconscious mind is a compilation of all the things you have experienced since you were young. Your subconscious mind acts as a "storehouse" of everything you have gone through in your life. These things affect the way you think and the way you do things.

You may not be aware of it, but there are things there in your mind that dictates your every action, which are far different from what you consciously think about. So if you have, at some point in your life, found that a more simplistic lifestyle is far better than a financially well-off lifestyle, then you may have a challenge trying to acquire wealth. If you have experienced the acquisition of money as being not a good thing, then you may have a difficulty getting your first million.

Achieving a millionaire mind takes a lot of work and involves the undoing of limiting that you have acquired over the years. It can be done, but you will need to find the right tools to help you. Once you start to think in a positive way about the acquisition of money, then it will become a whole lot easier to acquire it. In fact, you may find that out of the blue money is indeed coming your way.

Having a millionaire's mindset is in no way steeped in mystery. It is achievable to every human being if they want to achieve a rich lifestyle. What you think about is what you will start to see showing up in your life. We are a mirror of the world so if we start to think and act positively towards the accomplishment of acquiring wealth, then this will start to show up in your life. It may not be very noticeable at first, but life has a funny way of giving us everyday signs, and if we are "conscious" of these signs and act on them, then you will start to see the end results, which can be lucrative.

We all have a lot of dreams; some of us want to become a millionaire and some of us want to find love. Some of us want to have great friendships, and we want to live in a great environment that we love and feel comfortable in. Many of us want to succeed at work we do. One problem with the way many people see their lives, however, is that we see all the different parts of being separate, instead of as one whole. The truth is that all of the different parts are connected together as one. This is because they all have to do with how we see ourselves. If you have a negative self-image, you are not going to be able to succeed in any aspect of your life. In short, by developing a positive self-vision and believing that you can achieve the top, then you can become a millionaire and all other dreams you have for yourself.

This may seem like just another promise that will never be fulfilled. After all, there are a lot of services and tools out there that promise to help you become a millionaire. This makes it so important to choose the best techniques/methods. It begins, perhaps, with positive affirmations. These are little sayings that you can read or listen to, and they will make you feel good about yourself. You will be developing a positive self-image as you engage with these affirmations. If you want to get inside the millionaire mind, you have to start with positive thinking.

Is this all it takes to become a millionaire? If you have read this far, then you probably really want to know how to become a millionaire. Well, if you want to take it a step further, then you have to participate in meditation. You are now probably thinking that this sounds like some new age jargon. But the truth is that all meditation requires and is, is concentration. It's all about focusing on yourself and creating the image that you want to see. This is the secret to the millionaire mind. Don't listen to get rich quick schemes. You need to practice self-visualization.

In the end, if you want to become a millionaire, you have to focus on yourself and your goals. This is all about two stages. The first is that you have to know who you are. The second is that you have to know who you want to be. By achieving these two stages, you will be able to know how to become a millionaire and accomplish anything else your heart desires. You can find a business coach online who understands this and will help you to inspire yourself to achieve greatness.

Success Factors

If you want to be successful in life, it is vital to know the various types of success factors that can help you achieve your goals. If you are aware of them and keep doing them all, you will be able to achieve just about anything you want in life.

One of the most vital success factors you should always consider using is time management. As you know, it is quite impossible to turn back the clock. Once you've done something, it is difficult to reverse the doing. If you know how to manage your time it becomes easy for you to complete whatever that is important for the day. Time management also gives you more time to relax and enjoy your life. Start by looking at the hours in the day and set your priorities to the tasks that need to be completed. Don't try to do everything on one day. This will lead to discouragement. I keep a to-do list in my office and prioritize it every day. Things change and, adjustments need to be made. The one thing I always do is to make time for family and friends because they are my priority. Make your to-do list achievable, and you will be quite surprised how the to do, becomes done.

Another one of the vital success factors is learning to become disciplined. However, this aspect is not an easy one and cannot be followed by everybody. Many people have great difficulty being disciplined for many personal reasons, and they have trouble focusing on one thing at a time. However, if you want to open up a business, you must make sure that you have this code of behavior in your arsenal. If you don't have, there is a great tendency that you will meet failure before you can taste the fruits of success. As discipline is one of the most important success factors, you need to force yourself to insert this quality in you if you don't have it yet. Discipline has been aptly described as " the bridge between goals and accomplishment." You need to learn to finish jobs, not get distracted and focus on the task at hand. Stay with it, in other words.

Some people might say that being a hardworking individual means you will be rewarded handsomely since you are incorporating one of the success factors into your life. However, this is only true up to a certain extent. If you want to achieve success, working smart should be one of the next success factors to consider. When you work the smart way, you can generate wealth and prosperity more easily because you are not devoting your whole energy, but rather you are finding ways to simplify the things you do. If you have a large task that needs to be completed, try to break it down into smaller tasks. Incorporate some help when you can. I once had a huge spreadsheet, which required manual entry of hundreds of records. I asked my niece if she would like to earn a little cash to do the job. She jumped at the opportunity and saved hours of monotonous work which freed up my time for more important things.

Keep in mind that being goal oriented is also another one of the success factors to consider. When setting your goals, make sure that they are within your capacity to reach. If it seems like an impossible mission, you won't be motivated because you already know that you will meet a dead-end no matter what type of success factors you utilize in achieving the goals. It is also important to set a deadline or a specific timeframe to your goals so that you won't waste too much time dreaming rather than working. Be very specific when setting your goals. This will help you achieve them.

Having the right attitude should be included in the list of success factors as well. If you always tend to make excuses, you won't go far in whatever you set out to do. When you are an entrepreneur, and there is a problem in your business, you need to find a solution to your problem and not merely give up. If you can rise in the middle of the most critical situation, this means you have the right attitude. A good attitude is a "can do" attitude. You will certainly achieve success eventually when you are committed and don't give up when you encounter a setback. All in all, when you have incorporated these essential success factors into your life, it becomes easier for you to move forward and transform all of your dreams into reality.

CHAPTER 10

DEBT MANAGEMENT PLAN

Many people have experienced the overwhelming pile of debt that makes it difficult to get ahead. This is one of the major things in life that causes tension in folk's everyday life. When not addressed, debt issues can cause medical problems as well as problems in relationships within the family. There are some steps that can be taken to help with this type of issue.

This section will cover some areas of debt management and reduction. You need to know how to handle debt, what debt management is and how to obtain help and why help is important. The information will give some knowledge about debt management plans. This will assist you in your journey as well as for those that you may know that are experiencing similar issues regarding their financial problems.

A debt management plan arises from allowing financial debt experts access to your financial details and, having studied the difficulties you find yourself in due to the mounting debt; they produce a plan, which allows you to pay off your creditors. Where a debt management plan differs from you trying to deal with an escalating situation of debt yourself, is that the debt management company contacts your creditors and strikes a deal with them about how much you have to pay back per month to them. Most creditors not surprisingly, are happy to deal with debt management companies, as they know that with a debt management company involved, they have a better chance of getting money from a debtor on a monthly basis, albeit at a possibly reduced rate.

Another benefit of using a debt management plan is that once the company begins the process of negotiating with your creditors, the pressure of dealing with these companies is greatly reduced. Those telephone calls will stop as well as those threatening letters. The company that you owe money to will communicate with your debt management professional. The worry and stress will soon begin to dissipate.

Also when you put a debt management plan into place, the interest being charged and other charges get frozen, so that your financial debt does not escalate out of control any further. You simply pay an amount that you can afford, as judged by the debt management company and a timescale is worked out whereby it is estimated that the debt will be cleared.

There are multiple ways of obtaining a debt management plan, and a financial adviser that is willing to help you. To ensure, however, that you are well taken care of and that your interests are being considered first and foremost, it is advisable to work with a financial institution that has a proven success rate for similar cases. An excellent place to begin your research on such institutions is at Chase Saunders. Their website is an excellent resource that will provide you will important and useful information about the programs and plans that they offer their valued customers. Begin your research today, and discover how to change your life, or the life of a friend or family member, for the better.

It is becoming a difficult task to handle finances day by day. The time is changing at a fast pace. Today, People need to acquire a basic knowledge of their earning and spending. People rarely understand the importance of it in their new modern life. And that is why; people create a huge mountain of debt. It takes understanding to make a right decision at the time of financial crisis. Whether it is a small or medium-sized debt, it has to be cleared as soon as it can be. There are many plans to implement for clearing any debt. If you are unable to repay your payments, then you can apply for this plan. As, the Debt management plan is one of the best ways, which works properly for you. This plan is about a contract between the debtor and the creditor to manage all your repayments into a single refund.

It is a casual agreement between a debtor and creditor. A Debtor gets a relief because of reduced repayments for a fixed period. The time depends on your means to afford your refunds. So, it gives you the ability to retain your financial control.

People can implement this plan by a licensed debt management company. So, you would be having correct operations while pursuing this plan. The important thing is for a company to enroll you in this plan. That's your debts relief plan UK, which should be an unsecured. It means your loan has to be without any security. It is because then, the company can work in the best manner to help you well. It is a basic requirement to apply to the debt management plan.

As per the changing times, you need to be an alert to managing your income as well as your expenses. Sometimes, it is not possible to take care of small expenses, however; they can turn into huge costs. These costs could be the reason for taking a loan and your debts. So, try to avoid your unnecessary expenses and you would be able to preserve a good amount of money.

However, debt management seems a competent option to handle your multiple debts with ease. Many debt companies are managing these cases of debts, and they will offer you proper advice on this matter.

Debt management is an appropriate solution for the debtor who is looking to settle his debt. By this plan, you would be assured and motivated to pay off your repayments to your creditors. Reduced refunds provide you a helping hand to have manageable finances as well.

Benefits of Debt Management

Debt management plans are designed especially for those struggling to meet escalating debt repayments. By getting in touch with your creditors, the debt management company will request that your payments will be lowered to an affordable monthly rate.

If you're considering a debt management plan, you need to know all the details of what it will entail. Here, we have put together a list of the advantages of taking out a debt management plan:

Free financial consultation

You can receive a free financial consultation where the debt management company will discuss your financial situation in detail to find which solution is the most suitable for you.

Reduce your debts in an affordable way

With the help of a debt management company, you will be able to move multiple debts into manageable and affordable payments. With your consent, the payment can be set on a specific date each month, most suitable for you.

Freeze your interest and charges

Although this isn't guaranteed with all debt management plans, it is possible to set a repayment plan that isn't subject to change, either interest or non-payment charges. With this in place, you will be able to maintain your payments without the risk of facing further charges on top of your set schedule.

You no longer deal with creditors

Once you have decided to take a debt management plan, you won't have to deal with any of your creditors. The debt management company will do all the running for you and make all your inquiries to the creditors. They will even write and post all the letters to the creditors - making your role much easier.

Payment plan that you can stick to

Every month you will only have one simple payment to one creditor - the debt management company. This will make keeping up with your payments a lot easier as you won't have to juggle different payment dates, rising charges, and multiple creditors.

Frequent re-evaluation of your payment plan

Many debt management companies can set up a re-evaluation program if you struggle to make the new payments. You can arrange a meeting every 6 months to re-assess the payment plan and ensure you're able to meet each payment. If not, you can arrange to change or reduce your monthly repayments, with permission of course.

One payment a month

With only one payment required every month, you'll find it far easier to maintain your payments. Struggling to keep your mounting debts in order will be a thing of the past - the debt management plan will do all of the hard work for you.

If you are in debt, you most likely need a debt management plan to get you out of that situation before it becomes worse. Service providers offering a debt relief plans could help you to get back on track.

Going into debt is maybe the most gruesome financial ordeal that you can experience. Most of the time you probably have no intention of getting into debt, and sadly you discover yourself in that financial pit. It may be as a result of a financial opportunity miscalculation on your part or gross misconception. Whatever may be the cause it is necessary for you to get out of the situation before it gets unmanageable? As a result debt management help can be your first line of recovery and should be thought about.

To ascribe to a debt management plan some considerations should be made. The circumstance you are in, the assets you own and any spare income available are the three main factors to consider. Of course, if you are bankrupt then you may think about various alternatives apart from debt management plans. A general starting point is where you prioritize and sort out the most urgent debts depending on the income available.

A debt management plan is part of a contract that you enter in with your creditors bidding you for repayment. This is accomplished when you periodically pay the installments of the debt owed to a business that performs the debt management services. This company will share out these repayments among your creditors based on certain conditions. You will have to ascertain that the businesses you engage in carry out the services that are licensed by the government. You pay this service through direct deduction from the repayments or as a separate set-up or handling fee.

Because big debt could incapacitate most of your financial obligations finding a suitable a debt management plan provides the best solution in such a case. It is essential that you make a complete disclosure of the possessions possessed, creditor details, debts, and any income that could still be coming into the debt management business. This forms the basis for calculating how much you should repay. Also, the company will also get in touch with each of your creditors to set forth the terms of repayment whereby the creditor may or may not agree to the terms.

Ultimately with this strategy, it is important to maintain a strict monetary discipline to avoid making the circumstance even worse. For example, you may not default on the repayment plan otherwise the initial agreements will cease to be bidding. It may additionally be desirable to come up with a type of budget to manage the available earnings more prudently and stay clear of a reoccurrence of the debt. It may also be essential to find out about the other choices available apart from the management plan and this could consist of the specific voluntary agreements, administration orders, and debt consolidation. Certain companies provide advisory services.

CHAPTER 11

EMERGENCY FUND

What is an emergency fund? This is a question that is often asked by people who don't have one.

It used to be that people had job security. A person might hold a job from the age of 18 until he or she retired at the age of 65. Today it is estimated that an individual could have more than 1 career during a working lifetime, even as many as three or four. Today, many people are finding themselves without an income, due to layoffs, downsizing and lack of available jobs. So what happens when the car breaks down, or the refrigerator dies?

Why has one? The best reason is, so you don't have to put the cost of an emergency on a credit card. You will still have to pay for it, and it may cost you a whole lot more money if it takes you more than the remaining part of your credit cycle for that month to find the money to pay the bill.

How do you get an emergency fund? Each time you get paid, you put money from your check into a separate account for emergencies.

What constitutes an emergency? An emergency is something that has to be taken care of immediately. If an appliance breaks down, your fund might be used to replace it. I'm talking about major appliances such as a stove or refrigerator. I am not talking about things that you could do without, like a blender. We are talking the big-ticket items. If your car breaks down, or someone in another part of the country dies, you can use the money in your emergency fund to get the car fixed, replace it, or buy a plane ticket to attend the funeral.

What constitutes an emergency? An emergency is something that must be taken care of right away. If your refrigerator dies, that would be an emergency. If your car just won't run anymore or needs repairs to make it run, that's an emergency. Having to travel somewhere for a funeral is an emergency.

The important thing to focus on here is an emergency. An emergency is different than a want. The want can wait. The emergency can't.

Tips to Having Emergency Fund

You never know what is going to happen in the future. You may have a cushy job at the moment, but happens if you lose it? Do you have enough money to ensure that you and your family can live in comfort for the time it takes for you to get a new job? It may very well take you at least 6 months to find a new job and to make sure that you don't have to visit the soup kitchen during that time is a good idea. Here's how you can build up an emergency fund.

- Decide what you need for a rainy day. If you have kids and your income is the only source of money for your family, you need to maximize your funds. But if you happen to be a two-income household and you usually earn more than you spend, your savings can be less. To determine how much should be there in your emergency fund, add up all the costs, including the fixed payments you have to make as well as the fluctuating expenditures of food, etc. Multiply it by 3 or 6 and you will arrive at a figure.

- Getting a temporary job or a second job is a good idea if you want to build an emergency fund. As soon as you reach the figure, you can leave the second job.

- Sometimes all you need is a bit of extra cash and for those times, pawn gold New York is a great idea. Today, the government has many rules and regulations for pawn gold New York and that is why they can be a safe way to get money in a moment. Pawn watches NYC shops are many.

- Work as a babysitter for parents who want to go out for a few nights or a house sitter for a family that is going out of town on vacation and you can earn quite a bit of extra cash for your fund.

- There are usually lots of things lying around the house, which you don't need. Why not sell them online? Be it clothes, records or other items; you can make quite a bit of money if you sell things you don't need.

With a little creativity, having an emergency fund is not a tough job.

Every individual and their loved ones should take advantage of a savings account which will act as an emergency fund in the case that funds are needed in the event of an emergency, job loss, or even an illness inside the loved ones.

How much must you save within the emergency fund? The opinions between financial experts vary, but most think about that you simply should save enough within the emergency fund to cover between 3 to eight months worth of expenses. Via these 3 to 8 months worth of expenses, it is important to include fixed expenditures like the mortgage, but also the variable expenditures, which are included in the budget.

Where can you find the money in the spending budget to start an emergency fund? It is important to start little and find little and subtle changes in the spending budget to start saving. A realistic goal is to begin saving ten percent of the earnings. Saving this 10 % of the earnings could be an effective way to make sure that you're able to very easily discover the room inside the budget to establish the emergency fund.

Making little modifications to the budget for example avoiding eating in restaurants, or avoiding spending cash on frivolous items. For example, designer shoes, or even finding a lower interest rate credit card or a less costly house can all make a large impact on the amount of money inside the budget that is available to spend. Therefore, allow you to put this money in an emergency fund, which can also act as an alternative to utilizing credit when you find yourself in a tough financial situation.

You will need to deposit the money into an account that is going to provide you with the highest interest rate. Through speaking with a representative at the bank, you can make use of tax-free savings accounts, or high-interest accounts that may be utilized to create an effective method to make the most of your money. You will need to ensure that you're maximizing the potential of the money that you have made so a lot effort to save.

CHAPTER 12

INCREASE YOUR INCOME

When the economy is in a downturn naturally many people are looking for ways to both save money, and where possible to increase their income.

The obvious things to look at are in the areas of employment. With your job, can you seek a promotion to a different level, which will mean an increase in salary? Do you have skills that might help you find a part-time job to supplement your wage, even if only as a temporary measure? It might mean working for a few hours in the evening after your normal job has finished. It could be something that you can do on the Internet if you can find a niche. There are various ways to increase your income if you have the initiative. That bit of extra income could just be enough to get you by until some of your debts are paid off.

If married, there could be other ways to increase your income. Could your partner find a job, even if only part-time? It's surprising how often just a small but regular wage can make a big difference to the family finances. People of working age who are still living at home should be expected to contribute towards the costs of running a home, so work out a realistic amount for them to hand over.

If, unfortunately, you are out of work, as so many are in this economic climate, what steps are you taking to look for work? Someone once said that getting a job is a job in itself. That is so true. There are so many people often all applying for the same position that employers can pick and choose the best. You need to stand out from the crowd. Don't just rely on the job center, but put your CV on sites where you can register with job agencies, though you need to make sure the agency is reputable. Nowadays there is little excuse for not having a well-written CV. There is a range of templates which take you through step by step showing you how to fill in a CV. Send off letters on spec to employers you think might be hiring. If you are interested, say, in retail work, call in some stores on the off chance they are looking for staff. Above all, try to stay positive.

Hopefully, some of the above suggestions about ways to increase your income may be of help in giving you freedom from debt.

Even if you are on a good salary, with the expenses rising every day, all of us require sorting out an extra income to ensure that not only can they get hold of the money required to meet their daily requirements, they can also save some money towards a more secure future. While there are some options to consider with seeing an extra income coming towards you each month, let us look at some of the safest options.

The Internet and Online Money Making

If you are already working and have a fixed job to cater to, you will probably be able to offer only a couple of hours every day to increase your income. Under such circumstances, the Internet can be a great way to go for this extra bit of money. There are a huge number of business opportunities that you will come across over the Internet.

Consider options like affiliate marketing, Forex, stocks, and so on. While affiliate marketing and other such campaigns (like Pay Per Click advertising) can show you good money and yet lesser risks, stocks and forex trading can be quite risky and requires you to be an expert on the subject. If you are not very knowledgeable about these options, it is a good idea to consider educating yourself on them before trying them out.

The Right Research

Affiliate marketing can show you good results as well, but it might take some time before you can see good money coming in from it to increase your income. And if you are wondering about the stocks and forex, it can be a good idea to get in touch with a good financial investment company, work with them closely, and learn the trades from them before you plan on going solo.

These were some of the immediate ways, or short-term ways, to make money. However, if you are planning on improving your financial condition on a long-term basis, there are a good number of investment plans that you can always check out! These schemes can offer you great returns, helping your money grow with time. Some of these investment plans are very safe, and can even work towards an annuity.

For this, you need to sort out a few things. How much money can you invest every month after setting aside money for your expenses, and also some money for liquid savings? When would you want to see the returns coming towards you? How safe is the plan you are opting for? Will it improve your credit score?

And there are some other questions that you should consider. Get in touch with a good finance company to understand your options with regards to how to increase your income in the best possible way, starting today!

Attitude to Possess

There are commonly held attitudes that interfere with the ability to increase your income. Sometimes, you're aware of having these attitudes and where they come from. Often though you have no awareness of them and that is when they are particularly deadly. Then, they are unseen obstacles. You don't even understand what the problem is. Let's look at a few of the most common attitudes that get in the way of clients when they want to increase their income. Do you have some of these attitudes?

1) I don't care about money.

If you have the belief that you don't care about money, you're either poor or lying to yourself. You may have the image that is caring about making money also means that you are greedy, ruthless, or willing to do anything for money. These images cause you to limit your efforts to increase your income. Yes, these may sometimes seem to be truisms. However, believing a character limits you. Money gives you greater freedom and more latitude to contribute positively in the world. Keep your virtues intact and simply be a good businessperson when pursuing increased income.

2) I want to get rich overnight without any work.

This childlike fantasy can set you up for every "get rich quick" scheme in existence. You're better off to think of increasing your income as a long-term or medium-term project and to accept the fact that it takes a lot of hard work. What's so great about avoiding hard work anyway? You're working for yourself to improve the financial conditions of your life. Isn't that enough motivation to get you working? You might want to change this attitude into being cautious about any claims that you can get rich overnight without any investment of hard work.

3) It's not "spiritual" or ethical to want to increase my income.

There's an attitude-which might come from religious indoctrination-that you would lose your soul if you seek to gain financially. What gets lost in this attitude is that these spiritual teachings also state that it is the pursuit of money that is the problem- meaning that pursuit above all else that is the problem. Increasing your income doesn't imply the loss of any spiritual foundation. It's not mutually exclusive that pursuing increasing your income means you can't keep your spiritual and ethical foundation intact. In fact, having both is extremely powerful and can be a wonderful contributor to the world.

4) If I just do what I love, the money will come to me.

Yes, it is important that you focus on doing what you love and love what you are doing while working to increase your income. You must be realistic also though. This is a fine fantasy, but without the foundation of business, you could spend a lot of time, energy, and money pursuing a plan that has no potential for increasing your income. You need to ask yourself things like:

- Is there a demand for what I want to do?

- Are people willingly spending money on what I sell?

- Do I have business skills?

- Do I know how to turn this love into a moneymaking enterprise?

- Am I willing to do what it takes to turn it into a moneymaking enterprise?

5) I don't have to take care of the money I get. Somehow that's a "dirty" activity.

Another attitude that can get in your way is the refusal to manage the money that you do have. If you don't manage your existing money, why do you think you'd be able to manage your increased income? Managing your money and accounting for its income and outgo builds respect for the fruits of your labor. It is a self-respecting attitude. Cultivate careful money management and investment of your surplus and your chances of increasing your income radically improve.

These are just a few of the attitudes that are most prevalent and the biggest obstacles to increasing your income. Just because you have learned these attitudes and let them "run" you don't mean that you must continue that behavior. You can change your beliefs. You can take new attitudes. You can eliminate these self-imposed obstacles.

CHAPTER 13

LIMIT BORROWING

Every time you borrow money, it is best to carefully consider if doing such is the right decision. Borrowing money means you're in a commitment to repay it back within the given time frame. How borrowing such amount would affect your future finances is something you should consider. It will be smart to ask yourself these questions before borrowing.

Do I Need to Purchase This Now?

Most of the time, the things that seem necessary aren't. You can delay or postpone the purchases until you have enough money to buy the item. Doing the laundry yourself might help you save much money for you. If it is just for recreational activities such as jet skis or long boards, you can let it go by for now and save the money, because they are less necessary purchases. In fact, it will help you save up more money than expected because you will be more motivated to make the purchases.

Can I Purchase Something That's Less Expensive Instead?

When making big purchases, you always want to get the nicest of what you can afford. However, you can get pretty much the same results by getting a close look at how much is needed. For instance, if you plan on purchasing a car, you may consider spending three to five thousand on the car instead of seven to ten thousand. With a smaller amount, you can still find a reliable and decent car for less, and you save yourself an amount that you can use towards saving or investing in your future.

Can I Afford to Make the Payments?

This is probably the most important question to answer with full honesty. How this purchase will affect your ability to do things in the future is something you should highly consider. It may mean you need to take fewer vacations because you don't have the ability to save much money. Additionally, you may be very tight on that budget that it is making it difficult for you to do anything. You may come to regret the purchase, and wish that you could turn back the time to change your decision.

How Fast Can I Pay It Off?

When taking out a loan, you should focus and have a plan for repaying the loan as quickly as possible. It is essential to realize that building true wealth is more difficult when you are regularly paying interest to others. Turning this around and can help you earn money with your money; you'll be able to reach your financial goals. That is why carefully considering all your options before you borrow money is very important.

What Happens If I Can't Pay It Off?

You should also think about the long-term effects of losing your job is something that is possible to happen. This means that there will be extra pressure on your part to find a new job quickly because any delayed or skipped payments will affect your credit score. Depending on the industry you are currently in, finding another job might be difficult if you have a poor credit history. You need to consider and look for options on how you can pay this loan off should you lose your job.

People borrow money for various reasons: for fulfilling daily needs, for purchasing things, for financing college tuition, for paying mortgages, for starting a business, and so forth. The amount of money borrowed is also varied, starting from a few hundred to many thousands of dollars. Different needs of money borrowers have instituted several methods of money lending. Three of the most common methods of borrowing money are loans, overdrafts, and credit. How should each one them be used for getting proper and effective money lending? Keep reading short descriptions below.

Loans

Loans consist of four major types; secured, unsecured, and Credit Union loans, and Money line.

- Secured loans

With this method, the borrower should surrender security to the lender prior to borrowing money. The security may be in the form of assets or other valuables. When the borrower fails to keep up with the payments, the lender has the right to force the sale of the secured assets or seize the assets as has been written in the loan agreement. As this method is less risky than an unsecured loan, secured loans are commonly cheaper regarding interest. This kind of money borrowing is mostly suitable for borrowing huge amounts of money over a long term, for instance for home improvements.

- Unsecured loans

This method does not require you to surrender any security, hence giving greater risk to the lender. Due to that reason, unsecured loans commonly have higher interest rates, shorter repayment terms, and more stern rules. Penalties may occur if you fail to repay after the maturity period or even if you attempt to repay the loan before the maturity.

- Credit Union loans

This loan is regulated by financial organizations. The loan is provided by and to the members of the organization. Commonly, members of the Union share similarity so that they can bond with an organization. The similarities may include workplace, housing territory, membership in a certain association, and so forth.

- Money lines

This method is provided for unfortunate people who face difficulty in finding financial institutions around their area. The money lines are managed by the community to provide loans for people in underserved markets and remote areas. The money lent may be used for working capital, business purchases, startup capital, home improvements, property and equipment purchases or personal loans.

Overdrafts

You will need a bank account to have an overdraft. This borrowing method allows you to borrow money up to certain limit when your account has no money in it. This is surely an advantage for overcoming short-term cash flow problems. This money borrowing method is flexible as you can repay the debt when it suits you. However, overdrafts are better used for short-term loans with small amounts of money, as the interest rates of overdrafts are high.

Credit

Another method to borrow money is by purchasing on credit. Using a credit card or other credit arrangement, you can pay for goods or services in installments. With credit payment, you can get better protection for larger purchases, acquire instant gratification, simplify travel plans and build a solid credit record. However, this method also has some issues such as irresponsible spending, interest payments, credit score issues and penalty risks.

CHAPTER 14

MORTGAGE

When a person purchases a property they will most often take out a mortgage. This means that a purchaser will borrow money, a mortgage loan, and use the property as collateral. The purchaser will contact a Mortgage Broker or Agent who is employed by a Mortgage Brokerage. A Mortgage Broker or Agent will find a lender willing to lend the mortgage loan to the purchaser.

The lender of the mortgage loan is often an institution such as a bank, credit union, trust company, Caisse Populaire, finance company, insurance company or pension fund. Private individuals occasionally lend money to borrowers for mortgages. The lender of a mortgage will receive monthly interest payments and will keep a lien on the property as security that the loan will be repaid. The borrower will receive the mortgage loan and use the money to purchase the property and receive ownership rights to the property. When the mortgage is paid in full, the lien is removed. If the borrower fails to repay the mortgage, the lender may take possession of the property.

Mortgage payments are blended to include the amount borrowed (the principal) and the charge for borrowing the money (the interest). How much interest a borrower pays depends on three things: how much is being borrowed; the interest rate on the mortgage; and the amortization period or the length of time the borrower takes to pay back the mortgage.

The length of an amortization period depends on how much the borrower can afford to pay each month. The borrower will pay less in interest if the amortization rate is shorter. A typical amortization period lasts 25 years and can be changed when the mortgage is renewed. Most borrowers choose to renew their mortgage every five years.

Mortgages are repaid on a regular schedule and are usually "level," or identical, with each payment. Most borrowers choose to make monthly payments. However, some choose to make weekly or bi-monthly payments. Sometimes mortgage payments include property taxes that are forwarded to the municipality on the borrower's behalf by the company collecting payments. This can be arranged during initial mortgage negotiations.

In conventional mortgage situations, the down payment on a home is at least 20% of the purchase price, with the mortgage not exceeding 80% of the home's appraised value.

A high-ratio mortgage is when the borrower's down payment on a home is less than 20%.

Canadian law requires lenders to purchase mortgage loan insurance from the Canada Mortgage and Housing Corporation (CMHC). This is to protect the lender if the borrower defaults on the mortgage. The cost of this insurance is usually passed on to the borrower and can be paid in a single lump sum when the home is purchased or added to the mortgage's principal amount. Mortgage loan insurance is not the same as mortgage life insurance that pays off a mortgage in full if the borrower or the borrower's spouse dies.

First-time homebuyers will often seek a mortgage pre-approval from a potential lender for a pre-determined mortgage amount. Pre-approval assures the lender that the borrower can pay back the mortgage without defaulting. To receive pre-approval, the lender will perform a credit check on the borrower; request a list of the borrower's assets and liabilities; and request personal information such as current employment, salary, marital status, and some dependents. A pre-approval agreement may lock-in a specific interest rate throughout the mortgage pre-approval 60-to-90 day term.

There are some other ways for a borrower to obtain a mortgage. Sometimes a homebuyer chooses to take over the seller's mortgage, which is called "assuming an existing mortgage." By assuming an existing mortgage borrower benefits by saving money on lawyer and appraisal fees, will not have to arrange new financing and may obtain an interest rate much lower than the interest rates available in the current market. Another option is for the home-seller to lend money or provide some of the mortgage financings to the buyer to purchase the home. This is called a Vendor Take- Back mortgage. A Vendor Take-Back Mortgage is sometimes offered at less than bank rates.

After a borrower has obtained a mortgage, they have the option of taking on a second mortgage if more money is needed. A second mortgage is usually from a different lender and is often perceived by the lender to be higher risk. Because of this, a second mortgage usually has a shorter amortization period and a much higher interest rate.

CHAPTER 15

CASH IN HAND

Get a good understanding of what you spend money on before making your budget. It is necessary to know your household's total income. Each dollar you spend should be accounted for. You should never spend more than you have.

The next step should be to find the total of your expenses. Make a list of where all your money goes during the month. Try to cover everything that you spend money on each month. It is important to be accurate and honest with yourself. Include money spent dining out or on fast food in your grocery bills. Document all of your vehicle-related expenses, including insurance, fuel, and regular maintenance. For expenses that do not happen on a regular basis, calculate the monthly averages, and include those in your budget. Be sure to include every expense, such as a babysitter, a dog groomer, or an even storage unit rental fee. Try to make your list as accurate as you can, so you can get the best information for budgeting.

With an idea of how much your household brings in and spends each month, you need to make a working budget. Some items in your budget will likely be unnecessary. Eliminate them if your income can't support them. Avoid daily stops for expensive coffee shop beverages or fast food meals to save a surprising amount of cash.

Upgrades and improvements to your house can save money on your utility bills. Purchasing a new dishwasher or washing machine that does not use as much water as your old one can save you a lot of money over time. There are other options for heating your water, such as an inline or on-demand water heater. If your water bill seems a little high, inspect your home for leaky pipes since these can quickly add to your bill.

Update your appliances by buying modern, energy-efficient models. They can be an expensive investment at first, but lower bills will make up for it. For those appliances that you don't use often, unplug them between uses. You will start to see a difference in your energy use over time.

If you upgrade your insulation, you will be sure that heat is not escaping through the ceiling or walls of your house. These upgrades pay for themselves through reduced utility expenses.

These tips will help you balance your income and your expenses. This can help you in saving money. Reduce your utility bills with new Energy Star qualified appliances. Using these methods will help you better control your finances.

Are you a retired person facing financial difficulties? You are not alone; there are many people facing similar situations. Despite having pension plans, insurance and all financial hardship hit retired people badly. Due to age, they cannot work to increase the source of income. Those who own property can overcome the problem and bring in financial stability in life.

Here are three ways to get lump sum amount in hand and ensure a peaceful retired life.

Home downsizing:

If you are living in a large house and you do not require such a big dwelling place you can consider selling the house off and moving into a smaller apartment. You can get a good amount in hand by selling your home; and then if you purchase a small house or rent an apartment, you will still have a good amount of money in your hand. This money can be used to solve the immediate crisis.

The problem is when the property market is down you can find a good apartment to buy for the lesser price, but it is difficult to sell house fast. You can find cash homebuyers who purchase properties for instant cash. You need to find out a reputed investor so that you can get close to market value, otherwise downsizing for money does not make any sense.

Once you downsize, you can save a lot of money on tax, electricity bills and other such accounts.

Release equity:

This is another way to get lump sum amount or steady income from your home. Equity release information and materials are there to help you understand the tool. These plans are usually made for senior citizens. You can release equity or the capital value of your home and get cash in return. The lender may pay you a lump sum amount of cash or a regular monthly amount or both.

A lot of elderly people decide to release equity to secure their retired life. Many equity release plans are available in the market. Before going for an option make sure you have gone through all the equity release information and understood the plan.

Sell and rent back:

Sell and rent back can be somehow compared with home reversion scheme. Undersell and rent back program you sell your house and rent back it from the new owner. People who are investing in properties or buying houses to make money either by selling it or renting it are the right persons to approach.

There are active networks of property investors; you can get in touch with such networks and see if you can find a buy-to-letter in your area. While going for the sell and rent back plan, make sure you have read and understood the agreement properly.

The entire process has its own merit and demerits. If you plan to release equity make sure you have sufficient equity release information. Same with other options; do your research and choose the most suitable option and secure your retired life.

CHAPTER 16

PRIORITIZE YOUR DEBTS

The debts of some people have increased along with the extreme use of credit cards that some debts are even amounting to a figure they can barely afford. What you need to know are effective ways to get out of debt because even if you throw out your bills, cut your credit cards or hide them to the deepest part of your drawer, the debt would not go away.

You could decrease if not eliminate your accumulating debts if you read on the ways and tips that I have listed below. As you read along, part those you can do and will work for you on those things that could work for you and start working on them right away.

Stop getting new debt

The first and most rational thing that you need to do to stop accumulating your debts is to stop acquiring new debts. One of the basis, why you lose control of your debt, is because you keep on adding to it, so you should stop using your credit cards to finance anything.

You do not need your credit card to live and they only serve as a trap if you are already in debt. It will not be easy to eliminate credit cards from your life, but in the end, you would realize that it was a relief to let go of them.

Prioritize your debts

Debts with the highest interest should be paid first because it tends to drain off money that you could be using for something else, and this is one financial rule you should keep in mind.

It is better to pay off your debts one at a time, starting with the smaller amounts first to push you to keep up your good work once it gives you the sense of accomplishment.

Record all your spending

Writing down all the expenses that you did in a week can make you see where you can cut down your spending. You can avoid accruing your debts by actually knowing where you spend your money on.

Get a second occupation

You could pay off your debts, starting with those who have the highest interests first with the extra cash that you would be earning from your second job. You would know that you have paid your debts in no time when you tackle them one by one.

Cutting down all your expenditures and luxuries may be at hard at first, but it might save you from bigger troubles in the future. By following the ways to get out of debt above, you could free yourself from financial miseries that have imprisoned you for so long.

When it seems that you have more debts than your hands can handle, then you need to learn the debt-juggling trick called prioritizing. Prioritizing your debts is foundational to paying them off as quickly as possible. You have to become more skillful in knowing which bills get paid this month and which ones will have to wait. Prioritizing is the DIY method of debt management. It gives you a way to make more effective use of the money you are using to pay off debts by concentrating on retiring one debt at a time.

1. Do your paperwork first

Get accurate, up to date data on each of your debts. If you are not sure, contact your creditors to give you the information. Write down the interest rates, balances, and minimum monthly payments for each debt you have. Also, write out the terms and conditions of each debt. For example, some loans have prepayment penalties that make paying them off quickly less cost-effective.

2. Arrange them with the highest effective interest rate. Note: Interest payment on mortgages or student loans are less than the stated interest rate because interest on these loans is tax-deductible.

The effective rate is calculated by multiplying the stated interest rate by the difference between 1 and your income tax bracket as in the example below.

For 30% tax bracket, and a mortgage of 12% stated rate - Effective interest rate is $12 \times (1-0.3) = 8.4\%$

3. Work out how much of your monthly income you can afford to put towards clearing your debt. Use a tighter budget to help you to get more money in this debt-clearing account. Pay the minimum monthly payments on all your debts except for the one with the highest interest rate. Pay as much as you can above the minimum payment on the highest interest rate debt. Keep doing this until that debt is paid off then move to the next debt on the list.

All of us have limited incomes. And when our expenses begin to exceed the income that we are bringing in, we have to make choices. This involves prioritizing debt.

Before you can begin to prioritize your debts, you have to know what your debts are. The best way to do this is to take a piece of paper or a spreadsheet and start to list all of your debts. This includes things like your credit cards, rent, mortgage, car payments, utilities, tuition - everything.

Once you have them listed start to organize them by order of importance. The ones at the top of the list should be the ones that will impact your lives the most if you were not to pay them. If two debts are of equal importance, the one that should take priority is the one that is charging you the highest interest rate. By the time you complete this list, you will have a really good blueprint as to the order in which you should pay your bills.

Also, consider late fees in making your prioritization list. This is especially true with regards to credit card companies who have begun to charge exorbitant late fees. So, for example, if one credit card charges 12% with a twenty-five dollar late fee charge and a second card charges 10% but has a fifty dollar late fee charge, it might be better to prioritize the second card even though it has a lower interest rate. There are other things to consider as well. The important thing is that going through this process will force you to read the credit agreements on many of the debts that you have. You may be surprised to find what kind of liabilities you are subject to.

The best time to prioritize your debts is before you need to. Don't wait until your bills are starting to pile up on you before making your list. Doing this helps you a great deal even if you are not behind on your payments. It forces you to be aware of how much money you are spending. A large part of why many people find themselves deep in debt is that they lose a job or other source of income. But another large part of why people fall into debt is that they simply don't pay attention to the debts that are piling up. Before they know it, they owe too much to catch up. Keeping a prioritization list like this helps you to pay attention.

CHAPTER 17

SPENDING IN VACATION

Throughout the year, many families will start to plan to take a vacation that will include adults and children. Across the United States, in particular, families will travel to the beach especially during the summer time. Very large cash expenditure doesn't have to factor into account if you take cheap family beach vacations. While some vacations will usually take a decent bit out of your wallet, there are several ways to reduce the cost you pay.

One of the best things you can do to reduce the amount that you spend on a family vacation is to save the money ahead of time by developing a plan on how to save. The earlier you start planning a vacation, the more time you will have to decide where you want to stay, eat and how to spend your time with activities and entertainment. The more you plan, the better your chances are at cutting vacation expenses.

Hotels and Lodging

Many people will start to look for places to stay, either hotels or lodges before they expect to leave on a trip. Budget-conscious people will do this by researching online. Hotels and other accommodations will list deals on travel sites for rooms and are more likely to raise the prices during peak season weeks. If you plan to book the room at a hotel you want to stay, you can save more by beating the rush before the season starts or just about the time it ends. Depending on where you take cheap family beach vacations, the peak season or on times will vary. One thing to consider when booking your hotel room is to find out what the off times are. Usually, an off time will include the weekdays or weekends in early May and the mid to late September. Another thing to consider is that some off times will be weekdays before Memorial Day and after Labor Day.

Summertime is usually the months of June through Labor Day weekend and booking beach hotels will be higher during these times of the year. If you do decide to book out during the peak seasons on a beach, try to find the hotels that offer discounts for using their website. Many hotels in beach cities will offer discounted coupons to local restaurants and other attractions as a positive incentive to attend their hotel. Also, since you are spending time with your family, a good idea would be to check into renting a unit or house located on the beach. The cost will be instrumental in saving and spending more time with loved ones. Plus, if you find a place with dining facilities inside, you can save on the cost of meals by cooking some or most of them yourselves.

Travel

Are you planning to travel out-of-state or out-of-country? Consider finding traveling sites with discounts on airfare and rentals of vehicles. Travelling is one of the important factors for reducing the cost of cheap family beach vacations. Airfares are discounted when you purchase your tickets well in advance, saving you both time and money. By finding your tickets early, you have the added advantage of the flexibility and being able to change the date if necessary. Check for any packages available for your family that will include the price of a hotel and plane tickets to your beach city.

Gas prices across the country are not always predictable and are not something that should be ignored. Know what the traffic is like in the beach area that you plan to vacation in and decide whether you want to sit in traffic jams with your family or spend the price of gas. Most of the time people will not want to spend the extra money for a vehicle, but would rather travel by walking or riding rental bicycles. Most beachfront hotels will offer discounts to their guests on rentals of bikes and you can usually get them in sizes to fit each member of the family.

Food and Dining

During your beach vacation with the family, food will be a big expense and major factor. There are several ways to limit the food expenses though. As mentioned above, finding a hotel or lodging facility that offers a kitchen inside you can save a lot of money you would normally spend on eating out in restaurants or getting fast food meals. A kitchenette in a hotel room gives you an area to store and prepare foods. Instead of dining out for every single meal, you can get easily delicious meals in your room. Another tip is to bring easily transported foods with you if you're driving to the beach. In the time leading up to your departure, you can plan for what your kids and family enjoy, saving you time that would otherwise be spent on grocery shopping when you would rather be enjoying your beach vacation.

When you do decide to eat out, reducing costs for meals can be easy. Find out if your hotel offers continental breakfast for your family or any coupons to the local restaurants that can be tailored to children. You can also cut costs by combining breakfast and lunch (often called "brunch") into one meal if the kids are supportive. Carrying snacks like dried fruits to serve the kids when you are on the beach or during family activities will help to gain their support.

Activities and Entertainment

Activities and entertainment for your family on your cheap family beach vacations don't have to be expensive. You can control the amount you spend by reducing the costs of shopping for souvenirs and gifts while at the beach. Most people love to purchase things as memorabilia and keepsakes. Pay special attention to your shopping and try focus on small (remember packing for the trip home after your last vacation?) memory-prompting items instead of fun or funny gadgets and gizmos.

Activities will be abundant throughout beach cities and are not limited. There are usually many ways to reduce costs by taking advantage of free activities in the area. The best free activities will be located on the beach itself: swimming in the ocean, soaking up the sun, building sand castles with the kids and looking for seashells or other ocean items. If you're the type that enjoys sight-seeing, be sure to bring along your binoculars or a small and inconspicuous monocular to view the sights and also to keep an eye out on kids as they play further away.

If you have ever traveled, you know first-hand how expensive it can be when you add up flights, hotel costs, activities, food and the cost of renting a car. In today's economy, we are trying to save wherever we can manage to do so. Saving on your rental car is easier than you think, but you must be prepared. It is difficult to save if you wait until the last minute to find your rental. You must do your research and know your stuff before you reach your destination.

Start out your research with your insurance company. Find out what you are covered on with the car that you own. If your insurance covers you on rentals, then you do not need insurance through the rental company. This is probably the biggest way to save on your next car rental.

Another way to ensure your savings on your next rental is to check your travel schedule and destination. Let's say you are traveling to a big city, but there are things that you wish to see outside of the city limits. While you are staying in the city, you may not need a car to get around. You only need a car to get outside of the city limits to go and see the sights. If this is the case, you would only need your rental car for a certain amount of days, but not for your whole trip. Realizing this can save you rental fees on days you may not even get behind the wheel!

Sometimes you can save on your car rental just by going to an agency that is located away from the airport. Be careful, though. If you find an off-airport agency that is cheaper, you may end up spending more money just trying to get there from the airport.

Make sure you know what your total cost will be before picking up your car. The "hidden" fees can surprise travelers. These can include gas fees; drop off fees, additional driver fees, and airport fees. In many places, you can choose to pay a flat rate and not have to fill the car up with gas before bringing it back. Weigh the numbers and decide what is best for you. Check to make sure you can drop the car off at the same location to avoid fees. Very few places will allow you to drop it off at a different location without being charged extra.

You can always get better rates on your rental car if you book your reservation before you arrive at the agency. Many companies will offer special online deals that you may miss out on if you choose to wait until you reach your destination.

Finally, when choosing your rental car, choose one that will suit your needs. If it is just you traveling, chances are you will not need an eight-passenger mini-van. A small car costs the least to rent, so take advantage of this if you are able. If you have a lot of people traveling with you, try and go with the bigger car that has the better gas mileage or one that is cheaper.

CHAPTER 18

LOANS

There are many types of loans, and depending on your credit score and history and the purpose of the loan, you should be able to find a loan to fit your needs.

One of the most common types of loans is called a secured installment loan. These are used to finance higher priced items like homes and cars. A bank or credit union will lend you the money that you need to purchase the home or car, and then over a period (usually five or six years for cars and thirty years for homes), you will make regular payments or installments.

Normally, the payments will be the same amount and due at the same time every month, and by the end of the loan term, you will have paid off the loan and the interest. There are, however, exceptions to this type of loan structure especially in the mortgage industry. Some mortgage loans have been set up so that the lender pays a set amount every month for a short period of two to ten years. During this time frame, they only pay interest on the loan, and when the term is complete, they owe the balance that is called a balloon payment.

This type of loan is only feasible when house prices are constantly rising because if the house price falls then the borrower's balloon payment will be much more than they will be able to obtain by selling the home. There are other vagaries in the home mortgage market like ARMs, or adjustable rate mortgages, where the lender's interest rate changes two or three years into the loan.

Another loan type is an unsecured loan. These include money that is borrowed for more intangible purposes. Although some debt consolidation loans are structured like installment loans as far as repayment terms are concerned, most unsecured loans are considered revolving debt. That means that as long as the relationship between the lender and the borrower remains amicable and the account stays open that the borrower can repay and reuse their credit according to his or her discretion. These loan types include credit cards, bank overdraft accounts, and bank lines of credit. Typically, these products have higher interest rates than the secured loans discussed previously.

Drawing characteristics from both of the above categories, a HELOC or home equity line of credit, is a revolving debt that works much like a regular line of credit but is guaranteed by your home equity which is the market value of your home minus the remaining amount due on your mortgage.

Other loan types target borrowers with poor credit and include payday loans and cash advances, which offer consumers fast money for a very short loan term with very high-interest rates.

Those are the basic types of loans that are currently available in today's marketplace. Some companies offer most of these loans in some form or another while other companies specialize in one or two loan products. Before applying for a loan, consult a trusted advisor or professional in the finance industry to make sure that you are getting the best loan for your needs.

Due to a large number of loans available in the market, many people are confused what different loans mean. To help you out here are some of the common types of loans and what they mean:

Home Improvement Loans

These are loans that you take to raise the value of your home to sell it at a higher price. It's usually an unsecured personal loan; therefore, you don't have to secure it against an asset such as your house. In most cases, it's short-term (you repay it within 12 months-5 years).

While the loan is great as it helps you to improve your property within a short period, it tends to attract high-interest rates; therefore, you should do your calculations and ensure that you can afford before you take it.

Bridging Loans

These help you in completing the purchase of the property before you sell the existing home. They are designed for landlords and amateur property developers; however, wealthy and asset-rich borrowers can also borrow them. Although the loan is great as it "bridges" the gap, it tends to attract very high-interest rates. It also attracts many overhead costs.

To get the loan, you should get it from an FCA (financial conduct authority) regulated broker. The broker will not only advise you on the best bridge that is ideal for you, but he will also advise you on other options that are available for you.

Car Loan

This is a self-explanatory loan as it's very common with many people. It is the loan that you take out to pay for a car. There are many financial organizations offering the loan and all you need to do is to research and find the best organization to work with. The repayment period varies from 3-5 years; however, shorter and longer terms are available.

You should note that the amount that you get depends on your credit rating; therefore, for you to have an approximate value of the amount that you will get you should check your credit rating with a credit reference agency.

This is a guide on the different types of loans in the market. Before you take any loan always ensure that you can afford it. As mentioned before, there are many lending institutions that have different interest rates and repayment periods. You should always do your research and find the best institution for your situation.

CHAPTER 19

CREDIT CARD DEBTS

According to the Federal Reserve, the average household credit card debt as of 2012 was just over $15,000. The majority of consumers who use credit cards report carrying debt from month to month, and a growing number of people are using credit cards to cover daily expenses like groceries and fuel. No matter how much you owe on credit cards, you may want to seriously consider the ramifications of debt on your lifestyle, family, and future.

Don't Lose Control

Unless you are using credit cards responsibly and paying off debt each month, you are giving up control. Carrying a balance means you will owe money in the future. As your credit card debt mounts, you give up control of some part of your future income because it will be required to make minimum payments. Some people make thousands of dollars in minimum payments every month, just paying enough to keep interest from bringing their balance over the limit! Those payments are funds that could be used for other things like savings, vacations, home improvements and family fun.

Any debt can also have negative consequences on your future financial and professional status. Although proper use of credit cards can increase your FICO score and make it more likely, you will be approved for things like car loans and mortgages, a high debt-to-income or high debt-to-credit limit ratio can reduce your FICO score. Your debt can even cause problems in the workplace as more companies are running credit checks before hiring applicants. This is especially true for management or financial positions.

Benefits of Getting out of Credit Card Debt

When you learn to pull yourself from the mountain of credit card debt, you take control of your finances. Benefits for yourself and others include:

Saving money as you are no longer paying high interest on balances;

Ability to budget money and spend on items you need or would like rather than pay credit card bills;

Higher credit score increases options for you and your family;

Reduced financial stress that can reduce tension in relationships and other areas of your life; and open credit balances that can be used for emergencies

What is Credit Card Debt?

For this report, credit card debt refers to any revolving credit line. In addition to the top players like Visa, MasterCard, Discover and American Express, credit cards can also refer to brand and store accounts. Department stores, gas stations, and online merchants all offer such accounts.

Tips for Getting out of Credit Card Debt

Tip 1: Define Your Debt

It surprises the number of people who skip this critical first step. They decide to get out of debt and begin making extra payments willy-nilly on their cards. They may solve the problem eventually, but they don't always go about it in the most efficient manner.

Knowing what you owe and how you owe it is a critical step in a debt reduction plan. Gather all your credit card statements for a single month. Using a piece of paper, record the total balance for each card, along with minimum payment information and the interest rate. This information will help you create an efficient payoff plan.

Choose one card and make extra payments on it while you maintain minimum payments on all others. You can choose the card with the highest interest rate in order to save the most money on your debt payoff plan. However, many financial experts advise that you start with the smallest balance. You will be able to pay this off faster, giving yourself a feeling of accomplishment.

Tip 2: Create Momentum

Regardless of which card you pay off first, once you reach a zero balance, transfer your efforts to another card. Keep paying the minimum on all other cards, but add what you were paying for card one to card two. This creates momentum. Here is an example, using three cards:

++++Card 1, Card 2, Card 3

Payments made while working on Card 1: $400, $100, $125

Payments made while working on Card 2: $0, $500, $125

Payments made while working on Card 3: $0, $0, $625

You can see that by the time you are working on card three, you are paying over four times the minimum payment!

Tip 3: Avoid Recreating the Problem

Many people can reduce credit card debt only to max out cards six months later. To avoid recreating the problem, you need to change how you think about credit card debt. Never use credit cards to pay for luxury items if you don't have cash on hand to pay off the balance. If you don't have the cash, you don't need the item. Pay off balances as soon as possible and only keep one or two cards open to reduce spending temptations.

A Common Obstacle to Getting out of Credit Card Debt

One of the biggest obstacles many people face when dealing with credit card debt is the constant emergency. They use all their funds to pay down debt. When the car breaks, medical bills arrive or another emergency comes up, they are forced to pay with a credit card. The best way to avoid this obstacle is to plan ahead. Before and during the time you start reducing credit card debt, create a savings account for rainy days. You should save a minimum of $1,000. You will be even more stable if you save a few months' worth of expenses.

Paying off credit card debt is not an easy thing to accomplish, but you will gain so many benefits. You will take control of your life, your future, and your finances, reducing stress and increasing the overall quality of life. Get started today by defining what you own and creating a plan to pay it down.

Credit card debt is not a national issue; it is, in fact, a problem that affects millions worldwide. Many of the country's population, especially the younger ones, get entangled in this problem due to excessive spending that is not aligned with their earnings. When you have more than one credit card account with overflowing balances that need to be settled but you are struggling with, then you are officially stuck in this complication as well. Having a few credit card accounts might not be too bad if you pay your dues consistently, but miss a few payments and your credit score would start to see the damage. Thus you are in reality affecting your overall financial situation as having a poor credit score would harm your ability to obtain loans with better financial terms in the future, for instance for the purchase of a home. Thus if you are facing credit card debt issues, the most natural thing to do is to seek credit card debt relief assistance! There are a few solutions out there for you when we speak of credit card debt relief, thus take your time to evaluate all your options. Weigh the benefits and disadvantages of each option, and then decide on what would be the best move for you.

One of the most effective solutions out there for those needing help with credit card debt is the debt consolidation option. Consider having a few credit card accounts, each one of which you pay separate interest rates, annual fees, processing fees and other similar charges. On the other hand, consider a single account where all your credit accounts are merged under, you pay a single interest rate for this account, and you do not have to worry about all the other credit accounts at the same time. I am sure that option two would be more appealing to almost all of us out there. Option two is, in fact, the result of debt consolidation, a process that successfully combines all your credit card accounts into a single one for better management.

You could explore the option of debt consolidation by yourself, or hire a debt management or consolidation firm to help you out with this process. If you prefer to do it yourself, you could opt for one of the many credit card balance-transfer programs that are available out there, offered by almost all the banks and financial institutions in existence today. Through this option, you could transfer all your credit card balances (regardless of how many credit cards you have) to a single credit card account.

This balance-transfer program offers you a different financial institution (compared to your current credit card lenders) that would usually put forward a lower interest rate to attract you. The program also comes with a debt-elimination plan that usually takes between two to five years to complete.

Or you could alternatively hire a debt consolidation firm that would help you eliminate all your credit card debts effectively with the use of a debt consolidation loan. The interest rate that is offered for this loan would usually be lower compared to your current credit card interest rates. Thus you would naturally be gaining by opting for this solution. Nevertheless, before you put pen to paper deal with any debt consolidation firm out there, ensure that the company is legal and legitimate. You could accomplish this by checking the legitimacy of the company with the Better Business Bureau (BBB).

Very few people might have heard about the snowball effect before, but this proves to be a functional way of eliminating credit card debt as well for many out there. This method denotes that you could eliminate your credit cards one after another, starting with the one that has the smallest remaining balance. You could do this by paying off the smallest credit account first, and paying only the minimum balance of the other cards to be able to close off your first credit card account.

Once this is accomplished, you should have extra cash every month to spare for the other credit card accounts. And you could continue along the same path until all your credit card accounts are closed. This would help conserve your credit score better than the debt consolidation option, as closing too many credit accounts at once would damage your credit score without a doubt. Thus this option is one that you should consider if you are looking to preserve your credit score, especially if you are planning to opt for a bigger loan shortly).

Being able to negotiate is also important for you to be able to get the best deal out there, especially if you opt for the debt consolidation option to eliminate your credit card debts! Always get a few options as well before you pick the best, and all the best in your bid to clear all your credit card debts effectively.

Bad Credit Debts

Society always thinks that some people are prone to the syndrome of bad credit. But that notion is not true as it affects almost anyone it meets along its way. But, to be on the safe side, you have to be ready to follow some instructions that experts can give you.

Act for your financial security

In the first place, you need to understand that some of the things that appear on your credit report are erroneously inserted there. Therefore, you need to ensure that you only pay for what you got, not just what ended up finding its way onto your credit card mistakably. At this point, Credit Repair companies come in with its efficient services to make sure that the wrong items are cleared off your report, and you don't end up spending money on things you have not benefited from. This is not a task that can be done by anyone excellently; it requires real expertise and proficiency. Therefore, as you come to these experts, you are assured that you will walk away with the best results ever.

At the moment, you might have already been grappling with indigent credit scores that easily warn others not to lend you substantial loans. This is expected if you have not managed to bring in the experts of credit repair. But once you bring Credit Repair Houston on board, you are assured that they would readily stand up and fix your credit score to make sure that you get back on track and continue enjoying your loans as before. If you have just managed to get your name cleared, that can be a great and excellent relief. But it would not be of any benefit of after being cleared of some of the large transactions; your score remains with very minimal improvement. Therefore, helping you to improve your credit score is just one of the best options.

End the nightmare right now

The very fact that your credit has reached an alarming level can scare you to the end of even causing a seizure. But not to worry because Credit Repair Houston understands every technique required sorting out such a matter. This is not only for the sake of making sure that your name is cleared but also to make sure in future you will be able to prevent such a thing from happening. Giving information you need to succeed does this. In the end, you will even have an opportunity of resolving the burden of bad credit that hangs over you. At the same time, your name will no longer scare people and organizations trying to offer you items on credit. But of all the advantages you can think of, moving around with a free mind is by far the most important and valuable. Otherwise, in some cases when you have too much of the unresolved credit, you might even find it difficult to introduce yourself to people who may eventually have an idea about your situation. Work with the best firm around that can fix and resolve your credit issues successfully.

Secured Financing

The problem of higher interest rates has risen, and it has become a fundamental problem since the cost of buying a new home has become difficult for homebuyers. It is also difficult for people with bad credit to find a mortgage for themselves. Individuals with unfavorable credit record have an option with bad credit secured loans, which has been prominent these days after the lenders have realized and supported the seriousness of the situation. Asking Guarantee

It is obligatory for the borrowers to present guarantee in the form of security that can be anything ranging from jewelry to home or any other precious thing that they own if they are applying for the bad credit secured loans. This happens to be an essential condition. Nonetheless, home as security is more favored in recently.

The total loan amount under the process of sanctioning to the borrowers is based on the assessment of the cost of the produced security has been adequately evaluated and calculated. Largely, the amount of cash that has been granted for the loan is around £3,000. This quantity can go up to £75,000 at maximum level. The period for availing the benefit of the credit ranges from 5 – 25 years.

Value of the Fund

The sanctioned fund can be invested in anything, and it has no fixed value. Home enhancement and reconstruction, business funding, children's improved schooling, purchasing car, etc., are few of the basic examples of poor recognition protected credits.

Nevertheless, the essential thing is that those individuals who take credit from others can employ and utilize the loan-sanctioned money for paying off the amounts, which are due to them. Due to this, their extra earning or value can come back to normal. In this whole process, there is no dearth of lenders for bad credits secured loans as the bazaar of money is filled with those people who let you borrow money.

Considering the bank account on lenders' purposes of safe instantaneous cash, loans available online is taken as the finest employing instrument nowadays. Presently, we can see many people who let other people borrow money from them according to their choices and circumstances. Those people, who let others borrow, reveal their regulations and rules according to their choosing.

This means that to escape from such kind of situation, it is required that at all times people should consume their valuable time while choosing a proper lender. Keeping that in mind, always go for those lenders whose rules and regulations are suitable for your budget and those who offer you the best deal of your choice.

Unsecured Loans

To the degree that we see it, an individual who is already in misery from an unfavorable credit record will indeed face some problems in receiving funds for his requirements. What people do not comprehend is that these are prospects that are an advantage to get hold of trouble-free finances. To benefit from the bad credit unsecured loans an assurance is not only necessary but this also makes it much easier and simpler to achieve.

Easy to Getting

Getting hold of bad credit unsecured loans can be an extremely straightforward job, as the person borrowing is not necessarily required to engage any guarantee of the credit. As we need to ensure with something to the lender, it becomes uncomplicated for borrowers like leaseholders and non-homeowners, since they do not include any positive feature to show, and it is accessible for all types of people wanting to borrow.

Prospective homeowners like people with debts or other bulky or with CCJs and IVAs who can't show their property as guarantee can also take up these unsecured funding.

Purpose of the Loan

The individual can take these unsecured loans for anything as long as the need of the loan is fulfilling. The needs can be anything from home improvement to debt consolidation to wedding expenses and even educational funding. These loans also can be utilized for car purchase and travel expenses.

Improving Your Track

By timely payment of the loaned amount, the individual lending can also enhance the credit monitor and add positive features to the credit history. In the course of this, the person borrowing can engage in a total variation of £1000-£25000 for the requirements. Because of unfavorable record of the individual, lending and guarantee-free temperament of the finance, the person is required to service the loan at a high charge of interest, yet a modest one. To benefit from lower interest rates, the person can adopt a study online. This will help him evaluate all the arrangements that are accessible to him.

Currently, too many lenders are available online and are all set to lessen their charges of interest owing to the hard rivalry online. With this, the borrower can benefit and make an informed decision about choosing which loan agreement is paramount for him.

They offer a means to the person borrowing for developing their economic posture and advancing their credit record. Thus, bad credit unsecured loan happens to be a blessing in disguise for people with poor credit history and inability to offer security.

Debt consolidation.

Now, this is an all-new type of loan, which can solve many problems such as people with an awful credit history, or if someone is seeking to consolidate credit card or other debt, this loan is just suitable for them all. Whether one wants to secure credit card arrears or extra sorts of arrears, it can be devastating searching online heading to locate the paramount ones intended for your requirements and circumstances.

What is bad debt consolidation?

Bad debt consolidation means that you take all your debts and pay them off by making one single loan. This loan automatically has a lower, controlled and fixed rate of interest, a more appealing amount of repayment and a reasonable term. You will have only one loan to repay, hence, avoid having the multiple monthly tours to the cashier's office, stop having to deal with harassing collection calls from agencies, reduce your stress level and have a better sleep at night. The debt agreement at debt fix will help you to achieve all these benefits.

Bad debt consolidation mainly divides into two kinds: secured loans and unsecured loans. Secured loans require you to place a guarantee to get your loan approved. This is in the form of personal property (like your home) and with it, you can receive low-interest rates for long terms in which you can make your repayments easily. People who choose this dangerous debt consolidation method need to pay off significant amounts (credit cards) of debt or invest in a new project, like buying a car or a second home, taking an expensive vacation, etc.,

Deb Fix is highly experienced in severe debt consolidation issues and has helped many people to sort their financial problems. They have an outstanding reputation, as you can see from reading trusted testimonials from their clients. They have been satisfied with their services and have recommended them too many other people who experience financial difficulties.

The services provided with bad debt consolidation loans include information, assistance and free advice that will prove to be essential for fixing your debts. A debt management plan is a key to getting started with bad debt consolidation. That's why it is vital to consult a financial specialist who can find the right path to take.

Getting Rid of Bad Debt

Various financial firms have provided credit card debt reduction services. It tells us how to enhance business with financial stability and where to go for the best loan opportunities to start a business. It provides various wide ranges of advice and solutions with different financial circumstances. This free service provided by companies where people will get a free consultation and solutions to your debt related issues. In spite of the fact that in some circumstances borrow money from right places otherwise, you will have to face some problems in your further life. You have needed to follow some strategies like always put aside some money for essential items and also make some control on your spending money on lavish things.

You have the need to learn some more new things about Credit Card Debt management although if you will learn how to manage this thing, then your financial position becomes much better as you collate with your past. If you are struggling with your existing debt, then you have a need to make concern with some professional financial advisor however he will guide you how to come out of this problem. Don't think that you are alone facing this problem, however, there are a billion people in the world who are facing this problem. The main solution of debt problem starts with you whatever you can take help from your friends and relatives also.

Some financial experts usually organize seminars to get rid of this issue although these all seminars are free. You can easily join them and get the solution to your problems from these experts. Debt management is the fast-growing scenario in the whole world. Despite this process is not a cup of tea however if want to enhance your credit score and credit repair. Join us on our website although we will provide you the solution and provide you better financial stability with good credit score. Our professional experts have been working in this field for many years. Click here to know more and we will bring you to the other edge. We have been assisting to intensify your credit card scores.

Finally paying off your credit card debt is probably one of the smartest financial decisions you will make in your lifetime. Having a large amount of credit card debt is very stressful, and the inclination to eliminate this stress for a more peaceful lifestyle is a motivator to seek options that will allow you to pay off all incoming credit card bills. Paying off all the credit cards takes work, planning and time, but it can be done if you have access to the right resources and financial debt relief help.

After realizing that large amounts of credit card debt have become a major problem in your life, getting organized is the first step. Retrieve all current credit card statements from their hiding place and spread them out on a kitchen table or other workspace in order from highest interest rate card to lowest. Compute the total minimum payments for all of the combined credit cards.

The next step is to determine the minimum amount of affordable monthly payments to reduce the amount owed for the entire collection of credit card debt. For example, the minimum monthly payment that you can pay to alleviate credit card debt amounts to $500. The total minimum payment for each of your three credit cards is $300 plus an additional payment of $10 for each card. Subtract the number of total payments of $330 from your minimum monthly credit card repayment amount to discover that there is $170 left over.

Use the $170 remainder to pay off the highest interest card debt every month until the credit card bill with the highest monthly interest has been paid off and the debt from this one credit card has been eliminated. Once a credit card balance has been repaid, it is recommended to close the account and cut up this credit card to avoid accumulating additional charges and interest on the same card. You should avoid opening up a new credit card account to replace the old paid off account and avoid the aggravation of paying off your credit card debt again.

Continue to make monthly payments on the remaining credit card bills. Use the additional money saved from each previous monthly credit card debt repayment to pay off the next highest interest earning credit card. Avoid adding additional charges to the credit cards that you are trying to pay off and instead use cash to pay for items that you need. Continue this repayment strategy until all credit card debt has been eliminated.

It is recommended that you negotiate with current credit card companies to lower interest rates as much as possible. Another credit card payment reduction strategy is to transfer the larger balance and interest rates to a credit card that has a zero percent promotional interest rate.

Tracking spending with various monthly budget-planning tools helps to retain money earned through income reserved for paying off the credit card debt. The more money that is saved each month by cutting back on unnecessary expenses the more money you will have to use to repay money owed to credit card companies.

Selling items online or at a garage sale or getting a second part-time job are ways to bring in additional income that can be used to pay down debt. Notes to self about debt reduction goals should be written and posted in the wallet and on the refrigerator as ways to reduce spending by remembering your monthly debt reduction goals.

Paying off credit card debt requires willpower, patience, an outstanding monthly credit card repayment plan and the help of additional resources. One resource is to contact a third party that offers a debt negotiation or debt settlement plan that can help you get rid of your credit card debt once and for all.

CHAPTER 20

REDEMPTION FROM FINANCIAL CRISIS

There have been many companies and individuals who have suffered financially. This has caused a rise in the number of bankruptcies among individuals and small businesses. The sudden shift in the economic scenario has left many people with a lot of debts and no way to repay these loans.

Looming Financial Crisis

Fortunately, there are many organizations who are experts in Australian debt recovery, debt management, and expert negotiators who are helping people slowly sinking with too many debts and loans. The main culprit has been the easy availability of which has allowed people to take out loans and in many cases overextended themselves. When the credit crunch hit hard, they were just not in a position to repay the loan and the overdue interest. It is in this scenario that a debt mediator or negotiator helps by assessing your financial situation and then working out a plan to hold off your creditors. The most appropriate way would be to go in for a debt consolidation loan, which is a legal agreement set up between your creditors and yourself through the offices of a debt mediator.

Consolidating Debt Program

By making use of a debt consolidation loan, you will be able to get some relief from your creditors and also avoid declaring bankruptcy, which would affect your credit ratings immeasurably. Here, they consolidate or combine all your outstanding loans into one amount, which means that you have only one monthly repayment to be made. This loan is usually arranged through bad credit personal loan lenders who will consolidate all your debts into one single loan, which will be negotiated for repayment at a much lower interest rate. This saves you a lot of tension, as the loan pays off your most serious and urgent creditors while assuring others that there is hope that they will get their money back.

Future Financial Stability

Having decided that the only way to exit this financial mess is going through debt mediators; you will then have to fill in the necessary paperwork detailing the entire plus and minus points of your current financial status. This might include all your income sources, usual monthly expenses, and how much you pay as loan repayment; the list will also include the creditors and how much each is owed. After the application is reviewed and approved by one of the bad credit personal loan lenders, your debt consolidation loan will be sanctioned. The organization will usually allot a debt counselor who will guide you through this debt problem, till you reach some financial stability.

The financial crisis is an ugly situation that no sane person would want to experience because it comes with very drastic results that can reduce wealth and standard of living. Unfortunately, the recession is sometimes unavoidable. Unavoidable cases come as a result of bad government policies, unemployment, and unfavorable economic conditions. The good news is that human beings can find solutions to any problem they face, so when there is hyperinflation, it's still very possible to survive.

In the past, top countries in the world have witnessed several economic recessions. Their downfall also affects other countries, especially those that depend on them for the supply of goods and services. Just recently in 2008, America faced a similar situation, though the country is already making efforts to recover from it. If they don't employ the correct procedures, it is possible that they may witness the recession again. European countries are not exempted from this as countries such as Spain and Portugal are experiencing unfavorable economic situations. Greece is almost unable to pay its debts and Italy's story is also frustrating. If the right steps are not taken soon, these problems may even become worse. Hence, the EU and the American government are considering various bailout plans and strategies for reforming their economies.

One of the indicators of recession is hyperinflation. Hyperinflation is a situation where the prices of goods and services rise to unreasonable levels. The situation is usually caused by currency debasement. This happens because currency's value depreciates and salary earners find it more difficult to buy products since they have risen higher in price. In most cases, people doing business usually cope better than salary earners because they can increase the prices of their goods and services. In fact, those in the middle class face more trouble because most of their earnings come from salaries and since their salaries are not high, they are unable to get what they want during hyperinflation. Another problem that the middle class may face is that their savings will depreciate by the time they make a withdrawal. Interest rates on deposits are low at this time, so people who have been saving in the bank for years will lose a lot of money.

Unfortunately, economic recession lasts several years and government strategies to effect reformation can take years before the results are seen. The government may also face a challenge from the population unable to believe in their policies even when sounding great. Some governments still make things worse by implementing the wrong policies. For instance, printing fiat currency in high amounts will make the economy worse because this can cause inflation.

When too much money in the hands of people causes inflation, printing more notes is simply a bad idea. Instead, a better strategy would be to reduce the money in people's hands by implementing reasonable programs. More so, the government can increase interest rates so that people will be encouraged to do business, which in turn can cause economic recovery and growth.

When the economic recession is very severe, banks and the stock market do not perform well. In times like this, the people can react aggressively and cause anarchy. Survival measures such as hoarding water and staple foods increase and some people even look for defensive facilities such as guns to protect themselves if any alarm arises. In some other cases, the people may transfer their reserves to other countries where they feel their investment will be safe.

The recession is ugly and it's something you would not want to experience. It's necessary to pray that these problems will never occur. Apart from prayers, helping the government to implement the right policies is also important.

The financial crisis made many people tighten their purse strings and re-evaluate what was important as their mortgages, wages and stocks were all battered. Now that the markets are recovering people are beginning to spend once again, though still more carefully than before the crisis.

One of the main issues for every man in the financial crisis was housing valuation. Those with variable rate mortgages found themselves owing much more than what they paid for their houses, and many were unable to come up with the extra tens of thousands of dollars each year. But recent data shows that nationwide home prices are back down where they should be, in line with median household incomes.

Thinking of buying now that the market has calmed down? Find a mortgage financial advisor in your area to discuss what you are financially able to swing...that way, you know that you won't end up in foreclosure, as so many Americans have in the last few years.

There have also been many advances beyond housing. Corporations are once again turning profits. Much of this came at the expense of jobs in plants and stores, which helped to cause the crisis, but it also paved the way for recovery. And though no one wants to cheer for "the man," the fact that he is profiting means that we, the people, are making enough money to spend as we desire, not as life demands. Which is our next sign of solid recovery: consumer spending.

Consumer spending tightened during the recession in the face of layoffs, furloughs and the loss of benefits. But today consumers are spending. Some analysts complain that the extra expenditures come in the form of health care. Though health care costs are soaring, it is important to point out that dining, recreation, and clothing sectors are also seeing a rise in profits. The important difference now from before the crisis is that consumers are saving.

Focus on what you can Control

My friend Michelle asks the wrong questions. The other day she wanted to go to the cellular store on a holiday. She called the store in the afternoon to make sure they were open and found out they would be closing early for the day - too late for her to get there and have time to pick out a new phone. Michelle then spent the next several minutes asking me questions such as, "Why do they close early? Why do they bother to open at all? If they're going to close soon, they might as well have stayed home. It's just 3 hours - what are they going to do with 3 hours? Why don't they just remain open for their regular workday?"

Instead, she should be asking how she can fit a visit to the store into her schedule tomorrow, and how she can avoid having this happen in the future. And that got me to thinking: How often are we focusing on the things we cannot control, rather than those things we can control?

It's like the weather: Everyone talks about it, but no one does anything about it. This is because we can't do anything about it. We can't control the weather, but we can certainly control where we live. Hate the snow of the north? Move south. Don't like the summer heat? Move to the coast.

It's the same way in your online business; if you simply focus on those things you can control and stop wasting time on the things you cannot control, you will be happier and more productive.

You cannot control time, but you can control what you do with your time.

You cannot control the customer service given to your customers by affiliate product owners, but you can control which products you promote, and thereby increase the odds of your customers getting great service, and continuing to click your links and buy based on your recommendations.

You cannot control the economy, but you can control how you earn and invest your money.

You cannot control what your competitors do, but you can control your own business and thus your own destiny.

You cannot always control what happens in life, but you can control how you react to what happens.

Getting what you want out of life is all about controlling what you can control, and use it to your own advantage.

You control your life. You control whether you're doing the things you're doing out of obligation or out of desire. You control your destiny.

Forget the things you cannot control and focus on those things that are within your power to control. You'll find you have less stress and more success.

Many new currency traders just do not know and understand the fact that risks analysis and money management is important in currency trading. Many think why money management has to be so annoying when they hear the word money management. It's just this kind of behavior that gets average novice trader into trouble. Why is money management so annoying?

Getting into a trade is thrill enough in itself at first glance. This is what most of the novice traders do in fact think that the currency market will do exactly what you want it to do, and you will end up with a trade that can make you a lot of money. You seduce yourself into thinking that once you enter the business, it will be hunky dory. Everyone wants to make money and a lot of money.

You find out to your surprise for some reason, or another market is not complying with the plan of making a lot of quick cash and is not going in the desired direction. Then all of a sudden it seems that the market is not at all cooperating. Instead, it is going in the wrong direction.

The gut feeling was so clear and compelling when you had entered the trade. It was a sure thing at that time. The business could not go wrong in your opinion. Now it has gone so far in the wrong direction that you may have difficulty in getting out.

Do you know now that most of this evolution of a position gone bad has to do with you entering the market and risking real cash without having a plan, a stop, and a tested money management system before entry? What to do now?

Most of us do not think it painful enough to change our thinking and take sound money management seriously until we suffer a few losing trades to bring the concept home. Now many of us have faced this type of a situation.

What is the psychology of risk control? The psychology of risk control sooner or later begins with genuinely believing that you will benefit from a risk control plan. When you have mastered your psychology, you will experience less anxiety in your business and will be able to implement your business plan more consistently.

So instead of fearing a stop out when your selling system tells you that the trade has gone wrong, think of it as getting a step closer to the winning trade. Never risk more than 2% of your equity on a single business. So if you have a $10,000 buying account, the most you will lose on a single trade will be $200. By limiting your loss potential on each and every trade, you will reduce your level of stress and anxiety during trading.

As you gain confidence in your money management plan, you will begin to see the profits increase. Your pride will grow from generating greater profits from each trade. That increased pride will make you more confident in your abilities to become a successful trader.

Focus on what you Want

The principles and lessons below are necessary to help you move in the direction you wish. It may take some time to implement these entirely, but stick in there and the changes will happen slowly and naturally. Progress is always incrementally one step at a time; so following this pathway will help you to move consistently in the right direction.

1. You Must Focus Consistently On What You Want

You must only and exclusively think of what you want, at the expense of any other thought. This is because where the focus is, is where the energy will begin to flow. By focusing only and directly on what you want at all times, the creative energy can only move to the thing you want. If you are haphazard and always shift between wanting and not wanting something (i.e., the positive and the negative), you ruin the whole focus momentum and energy. It is like going down one road, only to reverse and go back up it constantly over time.

You must move in one direction, and that is the direction of what you want. It may be that this isn't achieved at first, in that some negativity appears. However, stick in there and eventually you will totally focus on what you want at all times. It takes mental training to bring your mind doggedly back to what you want at all times for the real success to be realized.

2. Focus on the Moment

Alongside focusing on what you want, you must keep your mental attention in the present moment. This means the energy is being harnessed, and more access to the subconscious mind can come about. This also allows you to assess any shifts in vibration (i.e., emotional feeling) because the present moment is the most stable mental state.

3. The Key Is To Control the Mind

There are two aspects here. First is to control your focus. The mind should only be in a present moment state. Bring it to this focus every single time and keep it there. The mind will willingly obey over time, and this will be the reality for you. Next, is to focus on what you want.

Sometimes we are not doing this without even realizing. We must become conscious of what we are focusing on, and only keep our focus in that one positive direction that allows for success. Positive thinking, feeling, and manifestation should be what we want, and we only put our attention on that.

Training your mind in this way will give enormous dividends over time. Incremental improvement of the level of control will come about, and this will make you the success you desire.

CONCLUSION

Thank you again for downloading this book!

I hope this book has been instrumental and helpful in helping you understand the concept of financial and debt management.

The next step is to make a short review of this book.

Finally, if you enjoyed this book, then I'd like to ask you for a favor, would you be kind enough to leave a review for this book on Amazon? It'd be greatly appreciated!

Click here to leave a review for this book on Amazon!

Thank you and good luck!